The Smart Guide to

Access

2000

Basic Skills

Also available from Continuum:

Morris: *The Smart Guide to Word 2000 Basic Skills*
Morris: *The Smart Guide to Word 2000 Further Skills*
Muir: *The Smart Guide To Windows 2000 Professional*
Weale: *The Smart Guide to Excel 2000 Basic Skills*
Weale: *The Smart Guide to Excel 2000 Further Skills*

Coles and Rowley: *Access 97 Basic Skills*
Coles and Rowley: *Access 97 Further Skills*

The Smart Guide to

Access 2000

Basic Skills

A Progressive Course
for New Users

PK McBride
and
Elle McBride

CONTINUUM

London · New York

Continuum

The Tower Building, 11 York Road, London SE1 7NX

370 Lexington Avenue, New York, NY 10017-6550

First published 2001

British Library Cataloguing-in-Publication Data
A catalogue record for this book is available from the British Library

ISBN: 0-8264-5647-2

Typset by PK and Elle McBride, Southampton
Printed and bound in Great Britain by Creative Print Design, Wales

Contents

About this book

About Access 2000

Access is the industry-standard database management system for Windows, combining the power to handle the most demanding data processing tasks with an easy-to-use graphical interface. Professional on-screen forms and report printouts are easily designed using a range of colours and fonts, and further sophistication can be added using macros to perform tasks such as checking data as it is entered.

Access is one of the Microsoft Office 2000 applications and as such can interface with the other applications, such as Word and Excel. Access will also import data in a variety of formats so existing databases may easily be upgraded.

Aims

Although this book is aimed at students on a wide variety of business studies and other courses, it is suitable for anyone who needs to learn about databases and their application through the use of Access. The theme of this book is oriented towards business studies students, it will be equally applicable to students on a variety of further and higher education courses as well as to the independent learner.

Structure

This book introduces the reader to the basics of databases and database design through a series of application-oriented tasks. The basics are then developed further through basing the tasks on the operations of one organisation, Chelmer Leisure and Recreation Centre. A series of self-contained but interrelated units takes the reader through the design of a database for the centre. Each unit comprises a series of tasks. As each new function is introduced, the book explains both why the function is useful and how to use it.

The approach does not assume any previous knowledge of databases or the Windows environment. However, readers who are familiar with the Windows environment (whether 95, 98, Me, NT or 2000) and, in particular other Microsoft Office products such as Word, Excel, PowerPoint and previous versions of Access, will find their road into Access 2000 much more intuitive than those who are not. Equally, readers who have some familiarity with other database products may find the database concepts introduced in this book easier to grasp.

The approach is designed not only to introduce readers to Access but also to offer them a conceptual framework for the use and design of databases that will encourage the development of skills transferable to other applications.

The units will give readers the confidence to perform and understand the central tasks concerned with database design, creation and maintenance:

❏ designing and defining a database

❏ designing and using queries, screen forms and printed reports.

Getting started

Readers who have not used a Windows program before should first read through Quick Reference 1, *Basic Windows operations*, which summarises the key features of the Windows environment, and then turn to Unit 1, *An overview of Access*.

Each unit opens with a summary of its objectives and the skills to be gained, and is divided into a number of activities. Each activity includes instructions on how to perform operations, and tasks that ask you to perform those operations. Series of related units conclude with integrative exercises that offer you the opportunity to practise your newly acquired skills. These exercises have minimal instructions.

This book may be used as a basis for independent study or for class activities. In either instance it is important to:

❏ work methodically through the exercises in the order they are presented

❏ take time for rest and reflection and break learning into manageable sessions

❏ think about what you are doing

❏ expect to make mistakes; think about the consequences of any mistakes and learn from them

❏ use the review exercises at the end of each series to test your understanding of the earlier concepts and exercises.

A note to lecturers and students

The learning material requires little, if any, input by lecturers, and can therefore be used in programmes based on independent learning. Students and independent learners learn by practising the commands and techniques.

The text is selective and does not deal with all of the features in detail. However, it does take students step-by-step to a level at which they can happily use the help provided by the Office Assistant to master further features.

Lecturers' disk

A 3 1/2" disk is available (free of charge to lecturers recommending the book as a course text) containing files of data for completing the exercises, plus the reports and queries produced via the tasks in the text. It can be used as a shortcut to avoid lengthy keying in of data and as a means of checking the outcomes of the tasks. The disk, or selected files from it, can be made available to students to allow them to check their own work.

Conventions

The following conventions have been adopted to distinguish between the various objects on the screen:

❑ Dialog box names, menu items and commands are shown as **File–Exit**, which means choose the **File** menu and select the **Exit** option from that menu.

❑ Buttons, tabs and icons are shown in bold, e.g. **Design**

❑ Keys on the keyboard are shown in underlined italics e.g. _Ctrl_

❑ Filenames, names of databases, fields, tables, forms, queries, reports and other items created by the user are shown in italics, e.g. *Membership*

❑ Text that you type in is shown in bold italics e.g. ***Aerobics.***

 indicates text that gives a definition of a term. Note that all definitions are also included in the Glossary.

 indicates a tip providing a helpful hint or short-cut method.

 indicates a cautionary note.

 indicates a cross reference.

An overview of Access

All students, except those who have some experience of Access, should read this module. *Quick reference 2* (page 134) reviews the basic features of Windows for the benefit of inexperienced users or as a ready reference. It also introduces mouse techniques and acts as a summary of the terminology used throughout these units.

A tour of the Access window and the Database window

It is worthwhile studying the two basic windows in Access - the Access window and the Database window – for a few moments before trying to use the program. This section can be used as a ready reference and returned to later as necessary.

The Access window

When you first start Access, the Access window shown in Figure 1.1 is displayed.

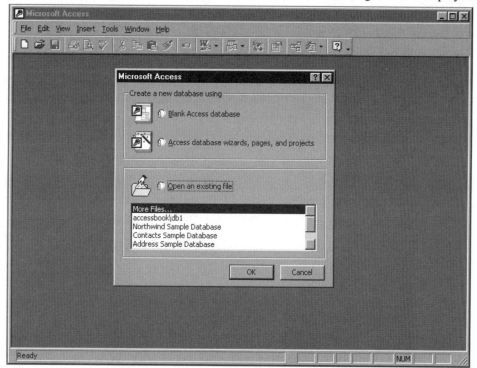

Figure 1.1

When this window first opens, you will see the Access dialog box, from where you can create a new database or open an existing one. We will return to this later. First, let's have a look at the other features of this window.

The window has the following components:

Component	Description
Title bar	Shows that you are in Microsoft Access
Access control menu (top left-hand corner)	You can click on the Access icon, to open a menu of commands for sizing and moving the **Access** window, and for closing Access
Access menu bar	Shows the pull-down menus
Toolbar	Shows the standard set of buttons
Status bar (bottom of the screen)	Shows the status of the system, and whether switches such as NUM for Number Lock are on or off

The Database window

Once you have opened a database, a window like the one in Figure 1.2 is displayed. This window allows you to access any *object* in the database by opening one of the sets of objects and selecting from there. The objects are automatically organised by type (table, query, form, report, etc.), and you can set up your own *groups* of objects. Initially the **Table** set is selected and the window displays all tables in the database.

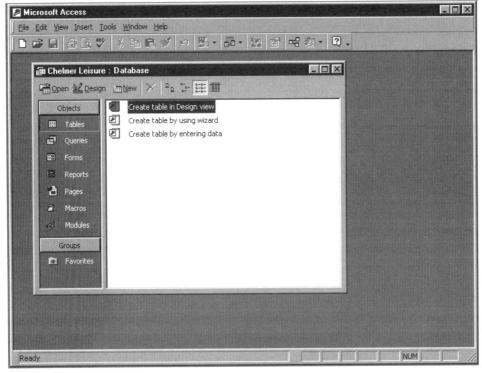

Figure 1.2

The Database window has the following components:

Component	Description
Title bar	Shows that name of the current database
Toolbar	Shows the buttons for working with objects. The buttons vary depending on the type of objects that are being displayed. For example, when looking at table objects, there are toolbar options for opening or designing existing tables, or for creating a new one. The four buttons on the right set the display style, and are always present. All toolbar choices have equivalent menu selections.
Status bar	Messages are displayed on the left of this, for example, *Ready*.

Help and the Office Assistant

When you start using Access for the first time the Office Assistant will appear to guide you. This is an animated graphic, with accompanying sounds.

When you have a question about how to do something you can ask the Office Assistant, for example, 'How do I create a query?'

1   If the **What would you like to do** box is not visible, click on the Assistant image to open it.

2   Type in your question – using natural language, e.g. 'how do I print a report?'

3   Click on the **Search** button.

4   The Assistant will offer several possible answers. Click on one to read the Help page.

What would you like to do?

- Print a report
- Set margins, page orientation, and other page setup options
- Set up a new printer
- Keep data in a record together on a page or in a column on a form or report
- Examples of printing orders
- ▼ See more...

how do I print a report

Options   Search

You can choose the appearance of the Assistant, and as this is shared by rest of the Office suite, it will be a familiar guide when you are working with other applications. To change it, right-click on the Assistant and select **Choose Assistant...** Be prepared to install the new images from the Office CD-ROM.

Hide

Options...

Choose Assistant...

Animate!

You can get into the Help system directly, without using the Assistant. If you want to do this, turn the Assistant off in the Options panel. To access the Help system then, use any of these methods:

❑   Pull down the **Help** menu and select **Microsoft Access Help**.

❑   Press the function key *F1*.

❑   Click on the **Office Assistant** button 🛈.

Click on a blue phrase for a definition

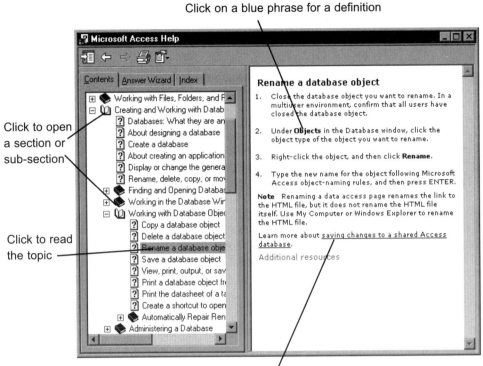

Click to open
a section or
sub-section

Click to read
the topic

Figure 1.3   Click on an underlined phrase to read the linked topic

These all take you to the Access Help panel (Figure 1.3). Here you can can browse through the Contents or Index, or ask a question through the Answer Wizard.

In the Contents section you may select any of the topics to find information about that topic. The Answer Wizard section enables you to type in a question, as you can through the Office Assistant. In the Index section you may type in a word that is matched by the index about which you can display information.

Other sources of Help

❏ Pull down the **Help** menu and select **What's this?** or press *Shift*+*F1*. The pointer will then have a question mark after it ⏳**?**. Point and click on any object to read a brief description of it. When you click a second time, the pop-up description box will close and the pointer revert to normal.

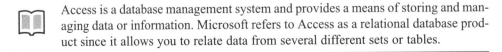

❏ Most dialog boxes have a ? Help button on the title bar. Click on this to activate the **What's this?** pointer, then click on the item in the dialog box to find out what it does.

What is an Access database?

Access is a database management system and provides a means of storing and managing data or information. Microsoft refers to Access as a relational database product since it allows you to relate data from several different sets or tables.

An Access database comprises all of the tables of data and associated objects, such as screen forms and report, macros and program modules and queries.

Tables

Access stores data in tables that are organised by rows and columns. A database must have at least one table.

Columns represent *fields* of information, or one particular piece of information that can be stored for each entity in the table. For example, in a client database, there might be one column for surname, another for telephone number.

Rows contain *records*. A record contains one of each field in the database. In a client database, there would be a record for each client.

Generally a table represents each major set of information in a database. There might, for instance, be a Supplier table, a Client table and an Employee table.

We will return later to the issue of how data might be organised in tables, and how relationships can be defined between tables so that they can be used together, so that, for instance, data from more than one table can be shown in a report.

Queries

Queries are used to select records from a database. Access has three different types:

Select queries are the standard type. They are questions that you may wish to ask about entries in fields. They choose records from a table and store them in a new table called a *dynaset*. Queries are specified by completing entries in the Query by Example (QBE) window. You can define complex combinations of criteria if you need to select a specific set of records.

Action queries update values in a database table. They can be used to change an entire group of records, as in, for example, the removal of all records for former employees.

Parameter queries allow you to change the criteria for a query each time you use it. Access prompts for criteria entries with the QBE (Query by Example) grid. They are a useful way of creating an environment for end users where users complete dialog boxes instead of a QBE grid (see *Access 2000 Further Skills* for more on QBE).

Reports

Reports are used to print information from a number of records. They can show the data from either a table or a query. In addition to records, they may show summary information relating to the records displayed. Graphs created using Microsoft Graph may be added to reports.

Forms

Forms can be used to customise the way in which records from tables or queries are presented on screen. They help provide a user-friendly interface for adding new records or editing existing ones. Subforms allow you to display related records from another table at the same time.

Controls are placed on a form to display fields or text. Text on the form acts as labels to controls and headings. Changing the font or adding bold or italic emphasis can change the appearance of text on a form. Text can also be shown as raised or sunken or displayed in a specific colour, and lines and rectangles can be added to give the form a pleasing appearance. Controls, attached labels, form sections and the form itself all have properties that can be changed.

Macros

Macros are a series of steps or keystrokes that you have recorded, and which can then be repeated by running the macro. Examples of the potential uses of macros are:

❏ to add a button to a form so that it will open a second form

❏ to create custom menus and pop-up forms for data collection.

Modules

Modules are programs or sets of instructions designed to perform a specific task or series of tasks. Modules are written in Visual Basic script, the programming language provided with Office 2000.

Task 1: Questions

1 What is the difference between a report and a screen form?

2 What types of queries may be used in Access?

3 What is a table? What is the relationship between a table and a database?

4 Give an example of when you might use a macro.

Defining a new database

What you will learn in this unit

This unit focuses on the creation of an Access database file. This file is used to store all the components of an Access database, which you will be creating as you work through these units.

By the end of this unit you will:

❑ appreciate the reasons for analysing data before creating a database

❑ be able to define a new database

❑ be able to retrieve this database

❑ understand that data is kept in tables and there is usually more than one table in a database

❑ understand that the tables in a database can be related or linked together.

Before a database can be created, careful thought needs to be given to the data that should be held, and in planning the way in which the data is to be organised. This is known as data analysis and you will be introduced to the basic concepts in this unit.

Data analysis

A database is used for storing data that can be used by a system. Organisations may have order systems, management-information systems, personnel-data systems, sales-marketing systems, etc. Libraries have cataloguing systems and information retrieval systems. In general terms, systems can be viewed as being concerned with taking inputs or resources, executing some form of regulated change and achieving results or outputs. Systems often need access to data to act upon their inputs; if this data information is easily accessible, i.e. via a well-designed database, then the system will perform well.

Data analysts or systems analysts are highly trained individuals who design information systems, of which databases usually form a major part. They use their skills to determine how to organise the data in the tables in the system's databases. It is not the intention of this book to teach analysis skills but it will give you a practical insight into the building of a database.

We shall be considering the database needs of a small leisure centre, focusing on the data recorded about the members. Paralleling this is an integrative activity, in which we shall consider the database needs of a estate agent, focusing on the list of properties for sale. In a leisure centre, the database could also record data concerning other aspects of the business, such as room and course bookings. In Access this information could be recorded in other tables in the database, and these could be linked together. This is beyond the scope of this book, but is covered in *Access 2000 Further Skills*, to which you may want to progress after finishing this.

A table generally holds data about one thing or entity. There are usually several or many instances of this particular thing, for example, the members of the leisure centre. A members' table would hold details about each member.

Records and fields

For each member there is a separate *record* in the table. Each record is composed of data about the member, such as name, address and so on. Each piece of data within the record is known as a *field*. In this first set of units we will see how the fields of the database must be defined – setting the size and the type of data each will contain – before data can be entered into the records. Fields are given names to describe the kind of data they will hold; for example, the field named *Lastname* will hold people's last names such as 'Harris'.

The field names can be considered to be the column headings in the table and each row in the table is a separate record. Each record in the table will have fields with the same name but containing different data.

Defining a new database

A database is used to store all the tables, queries, forms and reports that belong to the system. To begin with, a database will hold the tables of data needed for the system. Note that Access stores all of its tables, forms, reports, queries, macros, etc. in a single file, and that this file must be created on disk at the start.

Task 1: Defining the Chelmer Leisure database

1 Start Access by clicking on the **Start** button, selecting **Programs,** then **Microsoft Access**. If you have a Desktop shortcut icon for Access then you may double-click on it to start the program.

2 In the **Create a New Database using** area, choose **Blank Access database** and click on the **OK** button.

If Access is already running, choose **File–New...** and double-click on the **Database** icon.

3 In the **File New Database** dialog box select the drive and folder in which to store your database. If you do not change the folder then your database is likely to be stored in the *My Documents* folder provided by Windows.

4 In the **File name** box enter the file name *Chelmer Leisure*. Access will add the extension of *.mdb*. (You will not see this extension on screen)

5 Click on the **Create** button.

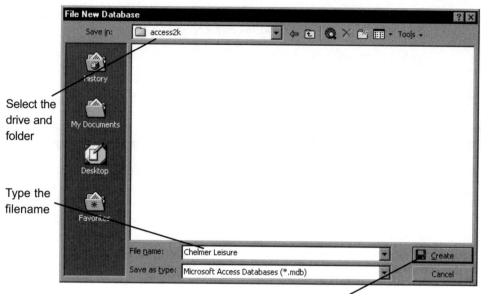

Figure 2.1

Click the Create button

Access, like other Windows applications, allows you to use long descriptive file names. The complete path to the file including drive letter, folder path name and file name can contain up to 255 characters. Any characters may be used except the following: * ? ; \ / : " 1 < >. You cannot use a period (full stop) except to separate the file name from the extension.

Closing and opening a database

When you have finished working with the database you can close it using **File-Close**. If you have made changes that you have not saved then Access will prompt you to save them.

To open an existing database use **File-Open** or click the **Open Database** button
. Select the drive and folder in which the database is stored, select the filename and click on the **Open** button.

When you have finished working with Access you can close it using **File-Exit**. Next time you start Access you will see your database listed in the **Open an existing file** section of the Microsoft Access dialog box. Simply click on it to open the database.

Task 2: Closing and opening the Chelmer database

1   To close the database choose **File-Close**.

2   To open the database choose **File-Open**. In the **Look in** drop-down display select the drive in which your database is stored.

3   Select the folder and then file *Chelmer Leisure* from the main display.

4   Click on the **Open** button.

5   To close Access choose **File-Exit**.

6   To open Access and choose an existing database, start Access by clicking on its icon or using **Start-Programs-Microsoft Access**.

7   Select *Chelmer Leisure* from the list in the **Open an existing file** are and click **OK**.

Defining a table

Having created the database, the next step is to create the tables that go into it. How do you decide what constitutes a table and the sort of data it should contain?

First consider the nature of the Chelmer Leisure and Recreation Centre. A leisure centre basically needs a building, staff and people that use it. Usage charges are often cheaper for members and some centres only allow you to use the facilities if you are a member. When someone joins the centre details about that person are obtained. Details about the staff that work at the centre will also be needed so that they can be paid correctly. Details about the bookings of various rooms, halls and courts in the centre will be required so that the building is used efficiently. If the centre has a bar or café then details about food and drink kept in stock would need to be kept as well as, for example, sales records.

We will focus solely on the membership data. What sort of information will the centre ask for on the membership form? Apart from name and address, date of birth is useful for targeting advertising to specific groups, e.g. senior citizens. Knowing about the person's sporting interests would also be useful. The information that Chelmer Leisure and Recreation Centre requires about each member is shown here.

Last Name	Occupation
First Name	Date of birth
Title	Date of joining
Street	Date of last renewal
Town	Sporting Interests
County	Smoker
Post Code	Sex
Telephone No	

Before issuing a membership card the centre will allocate a unique membership number, and will charge a fee. The centre offers different categories of membership for which different fees are charged. Therefore it is necessary to have two additional fields, *membership number* and *membership category*. When we create the table, we will set *membership number* as a primary key field, to make it a unique identifier for the member's record. We will look at primary fields in the next unit.

Choosing data types

The first stage in building the database is to define the tables. To do this we must define the fields that the tables will contain, giving a name, setting the size and selecting the data type for each field. No data has yet been entered but before it can be, Access needs to know what sort of data to expect. Take the member's last name. You need to tell Access the field name, i.e. *Lastname*, and whether the data is text, numeric, date/time, etc. before you can actually start entering people's names.

Every field in your table will be of a particular data type; for example a name is *alphanumeric text*, a price would be *currency* and a date would have a *date* data type. The data type that you choose for a field determines the kind and range of values that can be entered into it and the amount of storage space available in the field.

 You will probably define most fields in a table of names and addresses as Text fields. There are likely to be instances where a Text field should be used when the data is actually numbers. Fields such as telephone numbers or employee works numbers that contain only digits should be defined as Text fields. One reason is that there is no need to do calculations with such numbers. Also telephone area codes often start with a zero, and employee works numbers may also start with one or more zeros (known as leading zeros), which is not allowed in a true number. So, reserve the Number data type for fields on which you want to perform calculations.

The table below lists the data types available in Access and their uses.

Data type	Use for...
Text	Text and numbers. A Text field can contain up to 255 characters. Examples, names and addresses, class activity.
Memo	Lengthy text and numbers. A Memo field can contain up to 64,000 characters. For example, comments about a hotel in a travel company's database.
Number	Numerical data on which you intend to perform mathematical calculations, except those involving money. Set the FieldSize property to define the specific Number data type. Example, number of items in stock.
Date/Time	Dates and times. A variety of display formats are available and you can create your own. Example, date of joining.
Currency	Money. Don't use the Number data type for currency because numbers to the right of the decimal point may be rounded during calculations. The Currency data type maintains a fixed number of digits to the right of the decimal point. Example, membership fee.
AutoNumber	Sequential numbers automatically inserted by Access, beginning with one. Makes a good primary key field. The AutoNumber data type is compatible with the Number data type with the FieldSize property set to Long Integer. Example, membership number.
Yes/No	Yes/No, True/False, On/Off. Example, smoker/non-smoker. These are normally displayed as a checkbox, with a tick indicating Yes, True or On.
OLE Object	Document, image or other file created in another application. It can be linked into the database – in which case if its original file is updated, the changes will be reflected automatically in the database. Alternatively, an object can be embedded, putting a separate copy into the database, from where it can be edited directly. OLE objects can be up to 1 gigabyte in size.
Hyperlink	Clickable link to another file within the PC, the local network or the World Wide Web.
Lookup Wizard	Creates a link to another table, allowing you to choose a value.

Task 3: Choosing date types

Think about the following questions.

1   What would be the effect of rounding on currency (money) data?

2   What data type do you think you would choose for the following fields?
      Category No
      Lastname
      Street
      Telephone No
      Date of Birth
      Sporting Interests

3   Later we suggest that you use a Yes/No field for *Sex*. Explain this!

4   Why would you use a text field for a postcode?

Defining a new table

What you will learn in this unit

This unit focuses on the creation of a table. This requires the definition of its fields, giving each a unique name and specifying the type of data to be stored in it.

By the end of this unit you will be able to:

❑ name the component parts of a table

❑ create a table

❑ define data types for fields.

Defining a new table

In this activity you will define the membership table, setting up the fields so that they correspond to the type of data that will be stored in them.

Task 1: Creating a new table

1 The Database window should be active (indicated by a blue title bar if you are using the standard Windows colours). The **Tables** set should be selected as shown in Figure 3.1. If it is not, then click on the **Tables** button in the left-hand pane.

2 Click the **Create table in Design view** shortcut.

Or Click on the **New** button in the table window to display the **New Table** dialog box, then select **Design view** and click on the **OK** button.

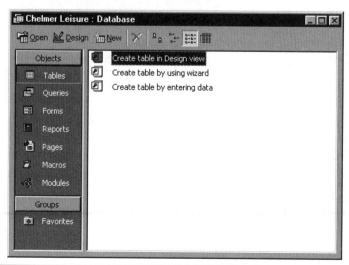

Figure 3.1

The **Table Design** window will open. This is where you define the table's structure.

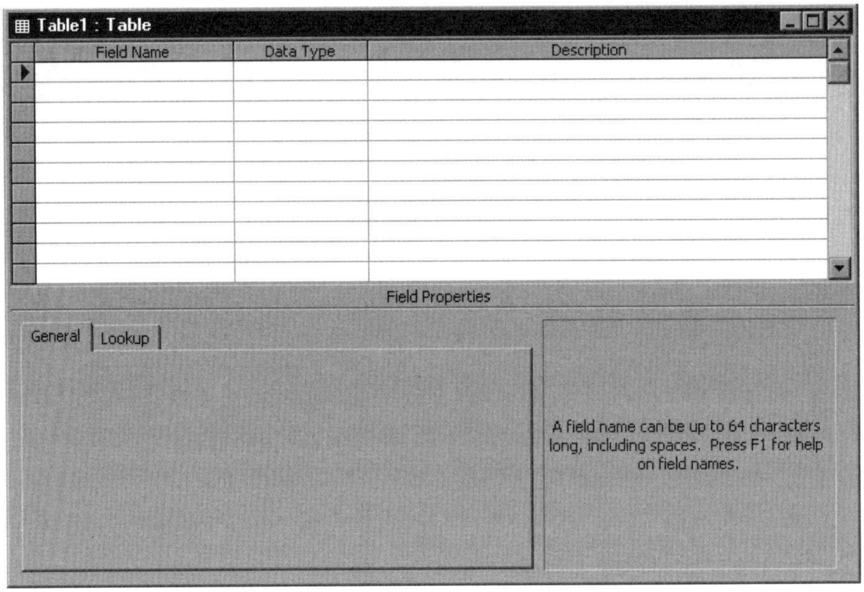

Figure 3.2

Task 2: Defining the fields in a table

In this task the fields for the membership table will be defined, by filling in the Field Name, Data Type and Description, and by setting Field Properties in the Table Design window. You should be able to complete this by following the immediate instructions, but additional notes are given in the activities described in the next few pages, which you may wish to consult. The table is defined as follows.

Field Name	Data Type	Description
Membership No	AutoNumber	Automatic membership numbering
Category No	Number	Categories are 1-Senior, 2-Senior Club, 3-Junior, 4-Junior Club, 5-Concessionary, 6-Youth Club
Lastname	Text	
Firstname	Text	
Title	Text	
Street	Text	
Town	Text	
County	Text	
Post Code	Text	
Telephone No	Text	
Occupation	Text	
Date of Birth	Date/Time	
Date of Joining	Date/Time	
Date of Renewal	Date/Time	
Sporting Interests	Memo	
Smoker	Yes/No	
Sex	Yes/No	

Table 3.1 Membership fields

1   Enter *Membership No* for the first field name.

Do not type a full stop after *No* as these are not allowed in field names (see the section on '*Naming Fields*', below).

2   Press *Enter* to move to the **Data Type** column and click the drop-down button, to display this list box.

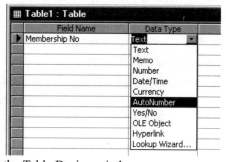

3   Click on the data type **AutoNumber**. Press *Enter* to move to the Description field. Key in the description as shown in Table 3.1.

4   Press *Enter* to move to the next field.

See below for details of moving around the Table Design window.

5   Continue to enter the definitions for the fields as detailed in the table. Where there is no description press *Enter* to take you to the next field name.

The table will be revisited later to set individual field properties.

6   The next stage is to define the primary key. Click on the row selector (see below) for *Membership No* and click on the **Primary Key** button 🔑 in the toolbar.

Primary keys will be discussed in more detail later.

You will save this table definition in Task 4.

Moving around the Table Design window

Through the Table Design window you can enter the field name, the data type and a description of each field (the description is optional) into the grid in the upper part of the window. To move between cells you have a choice of pressing either Enter, Tab the right arrow key or clicking in the required cell in the grid.

Row selector symbols

Along the left-hand edge of the grid you will see the row selector symbols. By clicking in the row selector box ▶ you can select an entire row.

Naming fields

Fields need names, lengths and data types to be defined. Access allows field names to be up to 64 characters long with spaces. Field names should be meaningful so that the data is easier to work with. Some characters are not allowed in field names: these are full stops (.), exclamation marks (!), and square brackets ([]) and you should note that you cannot start a field name with a space. You cannot give the same name to more than one field. Why not?

The length of a field (amount of storage space allocated to it) may be pre-determined according to the data type of that particular field. If the field is of a date type then it will have a standard length. Other data types such as text and number can have their lengths defined. If a text field is being used to hold the title of a song, for example, then you need to estimate the length of the longest song title and set the size of the field accordingly.

Adding a field description

You can add a description for any field in the description cell in the table's Design view. The maximum length allowed is 255 characters. It is not necessary to enter a description but it can be useful to provide additional information about a field.

Correcting mistakes in field name or description

Point and click in the cell containing the mistake. Correct the mistake in a normal fashion by inserting or deleting text at the insertion point. Click back in the current cell to continue working.

Correcting mistakes in the data type

Click on the data type cell concerned. Open the list and select the correct data type.

Creating a primary key

The primary key is a field or combination of fields that uniquely identifies each record in a table. As the main index for the table, it is used to associate data between tables. Though not required, a primary key is highly recommended. All the tables used in our system will have a primary key defined. It speeds data retrieval and enables you to define default relationships between tables. In the *Membership* table the membership number is the primary key; each record has a different number as every member's number will be different.

If the table does not include an obvious primary key field, you can have Microsoft Access set up a field that assigns a unique number to each record. This automatically numbers each record uniquely. See Unit 5 for more discussion of primary keys.

Task 3: Setting or changing the primary key

To set or change the primary key

1   In the Table Design view, select the field(s) you want to define as the primary key.

  ❑   To select one field, click the row selector.

  ❑   To select multiple fields, hold down the *Ctrl* key, and click the row selectors for each field.

Click on the **Primary Key** button 🔑 on the toolbar, or choose **Edit-Primary Key**.

Access places the primary key icon in the row selector column.

To have Access define the primary key

1   With the Table Design view displayed, save the table (see below) without specifying a primary key.

2   Access asks if you want it to create a primary key field. Choose **Yes**. Access creates a field in your table called *ID* with the AutoNumber data type.

Saving the table definition

Once the structure of the table has been designed it needs to be saved. Access uses this information to set up templates through which you enter data into the table.

The table is saved as part of the database file. There may be more than one table in a database file, each with its own unique name. Access allows the same freedom for naming tables – and queries, forms, reports and macros – as it does for files. A name may be 255 characters long and contain any alphanumeric text. Give your tables meaningful names so that they can be easily recognised later.

Task 4: Saving the table definition

1   Choose **File-Save**.

2   In the **Save As** dialog box, type *Membership* in the **Table Name** box and click **OK**.

3   Close the table using **File-Close** (shortcut key *Ctrl+W*).

Closing and opening the table

To close a table

1   Double-click on the table's control menu button.

Or   Choose **File-Close**.

You can open an existing table in either Design view or Datasheet view. So far we have only considered the Design view of a table.

To open a table in Design view

1   In the **Database** window, click on the **Table** tab.

2   Select the table you want to open, and then click on the **Design** button.

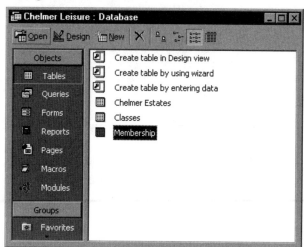

Unit 4

Defining field properties

What you will learn in this unit

Once the fields of a table have been defined, further refinements may be made to them by setting field properties. As with any computer system, it is important to keep your databases properly documented. The Documenter facility is a useful aid in this respect.

By the end of this unit you will be able to:

❏ define field properties

❏ create data validation rules

❏ define custom display formats

❏ print out the field properties.

Defining field properties

You may have noticed that once you start to enter the field definitions, field name, data type and description, then the Field Properties are displayed in the lower left hand section of the design window (Figure 4.1). You have defined the basic data type for each field and by setting the field properties you can specify the data type in more detail, for example, for *Text* you can define the length of the field.

General	Lookup	
Field Size	20
Format	
Input Mask	
Caption	
Default Value	
Validation Rule	
Validation Text	
Required	No
Allow Zero Length	No
Indexed	No
Unicode Compression	Yes

Figure 4.1

In the Field Properties section, in the bottom part of the window, you can set properties for individual fields to specify how you want data stored, handled, and displayed. The available options depend on the field's data type, and some will have default values set. When you click into a property definition slot, a description of the property is displayed to the right.

Setting a field property

To set a field's properties first select the field. Click on the property you wish to define and set the options as explained in the following sections.

The table below lists all the field properties (remember those you actually see will depend on the field data type), and the following sections describe some of these in more detail.

Property	Description
Field Size	Maximum length of the text field or type of number
Format	How data is displayed; use predefined formats or customise your own (see page 22)
Input Mask	Data entry pattern (advanced use only, see *Access 2000, Further Skills*)
Caption	Default field label in a form or report
Default Value	Value entered in a field when records are created
Validation Rule	Expression that defines data entry rules
Validation Text	Text for invalid data
Required	Whether or not an entry must be made
Allow Zero length	Allows you to store a zero length string ("") to indicate data that exists but is unknown
Indexed	Single-field indexes to speed searches

Field size

This property sets the maximum size of data that can be stored in a field. If the data type is Text, enter a number less than 255. This number should be chosen by considering the length of the longest text that is to be entered into the field. The default setting is 50.

If the data type is Number, the Field Size property settings and their values are related in the following way.

Setting	Description
Byte	Whole numbers with values between 0 to 255. Occupies 1 byte.
Integer	Whole numbers with values between -32,768 and 32,767. Occupies 2 bytes.
Long Integer	Whole numbers from -2,147,483,648 to 2,147,483,647. Occupies 4 bytes.
Single	Numbers with six digits of precision, from -3.402823E38 to 3.402823E38. Occupies 4 bytes.
Double	Numbers with 10 digits of precision, from -1.79769313486232E308 to 1.9769313486232E308. Occupies 8 bytes.

Default values

Access will assign a default value to each of the fields in your table, which is automatically entered when a new record is created. These are values that are usually appropriate for the addition of new records to a table. The default value for

Number, Currency and Yes/No fields is zero (No). Text, Memo and Date fields are empty by default. You can save time by setting your own default values for fields.

You can specify a default using text or an expression. For example, in an address table you might set the default for the Town field to London, if the majority of records are London addresses. When users add records to the table, they can either accept this value or enter the name of a different town or city. If, for example, an *Orders* table contained the field *Order Date*, then the expression *=Date()* could be used to put the current date into this field.

Validation

The data entered into tables must be accurate if the database is to have any value. However, even the most experienced data entry operators can make mistakes. To try to detect mistakes you can test the data entered by creating validation rules. These are simple tests, which are entered as short expressions into the **Validation Text** box.

Examples of expressions that can be used often relate to numeric fields, e.g. a credit limit that cannot be greater than a certain value. Fields with other data types may also be validated, e.g. a date may only be entered for a certain time period.

If the data entered does not conform to your validation rule, a message box will be displayed to inform the operator that the data is incorrect. The message is defined by the text that you put in the Validation Text box. The maximum length for both the Validation Rule and the Validation Text boxes is 255 characters.

If data in a record is amended then the validation will still be performed. If no rule has been created for a field then the data entered into it will not be validated.

Required entry

If the Required property is set to *Yes*, you will need to make an entry in that field for every record. Where it is not necessary to have an entry then this property can be left as its default value. In the *Membership* the *Category No* field has been defined as required, as a member cannot be enrolled without being given a category of membership. When you create the *Membership* table in the following exercise, consider which fields in this table are required and set this property accordingly.

Task 1: Defining field properties

So far we have not changed any of the field properties. In this exercise the field properties of the Membership table will be defined. You should be able to complete this exercise by following the immediate instructions, but additional notes are also given in the activities described in the next few pages. First open the Membership table in design view.

1   From the Database window click on *Membership* and click on the **Design** button.

2   Select the field *Category No*.

This field has a data type of Number and the Field Properties are preset as Field Size = Long Integer, Decimal Places = Auto, Default Value = 0, Required = No and

Indexed = No. The data that will be entered here is a number between 1 and 6 inclusive, as there are 6 categories. The **Byte** number type allows whole numbers up to 255 so is a good choice for the number property of the *Category No* field.

3 Click in the **Field Size** box, open its associated list and select **Byte**.

There are only six categories so a validation rule can be created.

4 Click in the **Validation Rule** box and key in *<=6* and type the text *'Please enter a category number between 1 and 6'* into the **Validation Text** box.

5 To prevent a number less than 1 being entered, modify the validation rule to read *<=6 And >0*.

6 Open the **Required** list box and select **Yes**. There must be an entry in this field.

7 Select the field *Lastname*.

8 Click in the **Field Size** box, delete the default size of 50 and replace it with *25*.

9 Alter the sizes of the other text fields as follows:

Firstname	*30*
Title	*10*
Street	*30*
Town	*25*
County	*20*
Post Code	*10*
Telephone No	*12*

10 Select the *Town* field again and in the **Default Value** box type *Chelmer.*

11 Select the *County* field and put *Cheshire* into its **Default Value** box. Why do you think these defaults are set? Refer to the section on defaults, above.

12 Select the *Date of Birth* field and in the formal box select the *Short Date* style from the drop-down list. Repeat this for the two other date fields.

13 Select the *Smoker* field and in the **Format** box replace 'Yes/No' with the *;"Smoker";"Non-Smoker".* This should display *Smoker* and *Non-Smoker* in place of the normal checkbox. Note it is important to put the first semi-colon.

14 Click on the **Lookup** tab then click the **Display Control** down arrow. Select **Text Box**. Click on the **General** tab. This is so the defined formats will be displayed.

15 Select the *Sex* field and in the **Format** box replace Yes/No with the format *;"Male";"Female"* which will display Male and Female instead of the checkbox. Set the **Display Control** to **Text Box** as for the **Smoker** field.

16 Save the changes using **File-Save**, and close the table using **File-Close**.

Creating custom display formats

Custom formats will display the data in the format that is specified regardless of the format in which it is entered. For example a display format can be created which will show all telephone numbers using a particular format e.g. (01777) 565656 or 01777-565656. A custom format is created from an image of the format. To design the image a special set of characters, known as *placeholders* are used. Here are some examples of custom formats.

Numeric format

# indicates a place for a digit, to be left blank if no digit is entered.

0 indicates a place for a digit and if the place is not used then leading/trailing 0s are to be shown.

, (comma) may be used as a thousands separator.

##,###.00	56.98 or	6.90 or	5,890.07	or	100.00
#0.000	12.456 or	0.020			

Date

d is the days placeholder.   **d** displays 1, **dd** 01, **ddd** Mon, **dddd** Monday.

m is the months placeholder.   **m** displays 1, **mm** 01, **mmm** Jan, **mmmm** January.

y is the years placeholder.   **yy** displays 01, **yyyy** 2001.

/ or – separates the day, month and year.

dddd d mmmm yyyy	Thursday 26 March 2001
dd/mm/yy	26/06/01
d-m-yy	2-5-01 (this format does not display leading zeros).

Time

h is the hours placeholder.   **h** displays 3, **hh** 03.

m is the minutes placeholder.   **m** displays 6, **mm** 06.

s is the seconds placeholder.   **s** displays 7, **ss** 07.

: (colon) separates hours, minutes and seconds.

AM/PM or **am/pm** displays time in 12 instead of 24 hour format.

h:mm AM/PM	6:34 PM
hh:mm:ss	11:09:57

Text

@	indicates that a character is required in the particular place.
>	Changes all text in the field to uppercase.
<	Changes all text in the field to lowercase.

(@@@@@) @@@@@@   (01777) 565656

Yes/No

;"Male";"Female" Displays Male for true and Female for false.

Task 2: Customising a field format

1   Open the *Chelmer* database and open the *Membership* table in Design view.

2   Select the **Post Code** field and put > in the **Format** property.

3   Save and close the table using **File-Save** followed by **File-Close**.

Documenting the table design

Access allows you to print the definition of your tables, forms, queries and reports. To get a printed copy of the design of the *Membership* table

1   Choose **Tools-Analyze-Documenter**. (You may need to install the analysing tools.)

2   At the **Documenter** dialog box, click on the **Tables** tab.

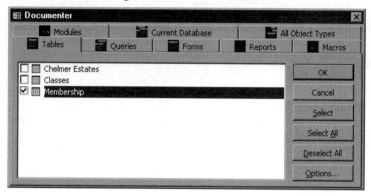

Figure 4.2

3   Select the table then click **Select**, or click into its checkbox to tick it.

4   Click the **Options...** button and specify the features of the definition that you want.

5   Click **OK**, back in the Documenter dialog box.

Wait! It takes a while to generate the definition for even the simplest table.

6   The definition will be displayed in the Print Preview window. Check that it has the information you wanted, and not too much – definitions can cover several pages.

7   To print the definition, click the **Print** button 🖨 on the toolbar.

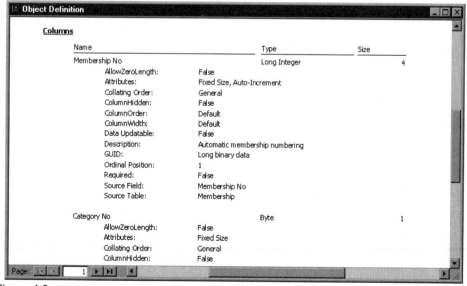

Figure 4.3

Task 3: Printing the Membership table definition

1   Display the Database window and follow steps 1 to 3 on page 23. Choose the *Membership* table.

2   Click **Options...** and set the following options:

    Include for Table: *Properties*

    Include for Fields: *Names, Data Types and Sizes*

    Include for Indexes: *Nothing*

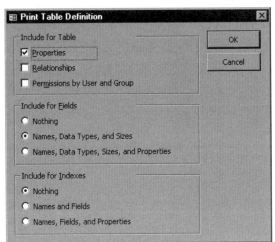

3   Click **OK** to close the Options dialog box.

4   Click **OK** at the Documenter dialog box, and wait for Access to analyse the table.

5   Print the definition.

Creating another table in the database

Access is a relational database system, and as such it allows more than one table to be created in a database. There is usually a link between the tables, but this is not necessary, and we are not covering at relationships between tables in this introductory text. (To find out about relational systems, please see *Access 2000 Further Skills*.)

We have included this new, small, table partly for practice in creating tables, and partly to give us someting simple on which to try out new techniques in future. The table involves another aspect of the leisure centre.

Task 4: Creating the Classes table

The *Classes* table is the second table in the *Chelmer Leisure* database.

1   Open the *Chelmer Leisure* database.

2   At the Database window, click **Create a table in Design view**.

3   Define the structure of the table as shown here, setting *Class No* as the primary key.

Field Name	Data Type	Description
Class No	AutoNumber	
Class Day	Text	
Class Time	Date/Time	
Class Tutor	Text	
Class Activity	Text	
Male/Female/Mixed	Text	

4   Set the field properties as indicated below.

Field Name	Property	Setting
Class Day	Field Size	10
Class Time	Format	Short Time (equivalent to hh:mm)
	Required	Yes
Class Tutor	Field Size	10
Class Activity	Field Size	10
	Required	Yes
Male/Female/Mixed	Field Size	10
	Validation Rule	"Male" or "Female" or "Mixed"
	Validation Text	Please enter Male, Female or Mixed

5   Save and close the table *Classes*. Print the table design using the same options as for the Membership table, and close the table.

↔   Data will be entered into this table via a form, which you will create in Unit 13.

6   Close the *Chelmer Leisure* database.

Reviewing table design

What you will learn in this unit

This is the first Reviewing Unit. Here you have an opportunity to check whether you have learnt the principles and skills covered in Units 1 to 4, and not simply followed instructions. Accordingly, this unit will tell you what to do but not how to do it. Only very basic instructions are given, which should be enough.

This unit reviews and offers practice on the topics:

❏ creating a database and designing a table

❏ defining field properties.

The Reviewing Units use a separate database, called *Chelmer Estates*, which is a limited simulation of an estate agency database.

Task 1: Creating the Chelmer Estates database and the Properties table

This task introduces the *Chelmer Estates* database and its main table, *Properties*.

1 Create a new database called *Chelmer Estates*.

2 Create a new table in the *Chelmer Estates* database, called *Properties*, to include the following fields:

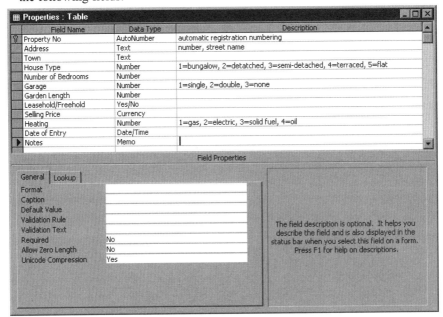

Figure 5.1

3   Save the table as *Properties*.

4   Access displays a message asking if you want to create a primary key. Click on **No**.
    If you do wish to set a primary key choose *Property No*.

Task 2: Defining field properties

1   If necessary, open the *Properties* table.

2   Set the Field Size of the *Address* field to 30 and of the *Town* field to 25.

3   Select the *Town* field and enter the Default Value of ***Chelmer.***

4   Create validation rules for the *House Type*, *Garage* and *Heating* fields, to prevent
    the entry of numbers higher than the valid numbers for their respective categories.
    Create corresponding validation messages in the Validation Text property.

5   Select the *Leasehold/Freehold* field and set the format to ;"Leasehoid,";"Freehold"
    instead of Yes/No (note: remember that the initial ; is important)

6   Select a date format for the *Date of Entry* field (we would suggest Long Date).

7   Save the table definition again and print the *Properties* table definition using the
    options set for the *Membership* table in the *Chelmer Leisure* database.

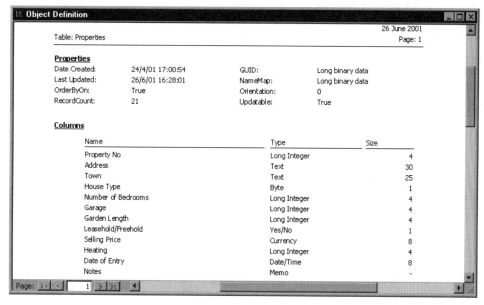

Figure 5.2

To print a more comprehensive table definition, choose the **Names, Data types,
Sizes and Properties** option for **Fields** in the Documenter, but note that this will be
nearly four pages long as all field properties are listed.

8   Close the *Chelmer Estates* database.

Entering and editing data

What you will learn in this unit

By the end of this unit you will be able to:

❏ display a table's datasheet and use it to enter data

❏ make a backup copy of your table.

Entering data

The next stage is to enter data into the table. Up until now the table has only been opened in Design view. To enter data it must be opened in the Datasheet view.

Opening a table in Datasheet view

In the Database window, click the **Tables** button. Double-click the table name or select the table and choose the **Open** button. The table will open in Datasheet view.

Once a table is open it is possible to switch from the Datasheet view to the Design view and vice versa. If you make changes to the design you will be asked to save them when you switch back to the Datasheet view. There is a button on the toolbar for this. Click the button to switch to the alternative view, or click the down arrow and select the view from the drop-down list.

In the Datasheet view the headings of the columns are the field names you previously designed. Each row in the datasheet is a record and as you complete each record it is automatically saved into the table.

Task 1: Membership data

1   Open the *Membership* table in Datasheet view.

Notice that there are some fields already filled in; these are the default values. A default value can be accepted or it can be overridden.

2   Do not enter a value into the *Membership No* but press *Enter* to move to the next field.

This is an *AutoNumber field* and if you do try to enter data into it the entry will not be accepted. When you press *Enter* after entering data into the last field of the first record, Access saves the record. Notice what appears in the *Membership No* field. Let Access number all these fields.

3   Enter the data for the *Membership* table as shown in Quick Reference 1 (page 127).

4   After entering the data for a field move to the next by pressing *Enter*, *Tab* or the *Right Arrow* key. When entering data for logical fields, click to set (Yes) or clear (No) the tick, or enter an appropriate word as defined by the format, e.g. *Male* or *Female*.

5   While entering the data, test the validation rules – both those that Access applies and those that have been defined. Entering a *Category No* greater than 6 will test the validation rule set up in the field properties for *Category No*.

6   Skip fields that are blank.

Validation, skipping fields and using Undo are described below.

7   Save the table.

Validation

Data is validated as it is entered, if it does not conform to the data type set for that field an error message will be generated. When the data entered breaks the valida-tion rule that has been set as a property for that field, if there is validation text, this appears as the error message.

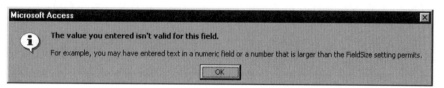

Skipping fields, null values

Sometimes not all the data for a record is available, for example, the telephone number may be missing. To skip a field, press *Enter* or *Tab* to take you to the next field. It is acceptable to skip fields where the data is not vital, but not for data such as the *Membership No*. Access automatically enters a membership number, as the field was defined with an AutoNumber data type.

Where a field is left without an entry it is said to be null, i.e. there is nothing there. If you perform mathematical calculations on numeric fields, then Access ignores fields containing nulls. Keep this in mind if you are doing any kind of statistical analysis. For example, if you could write a query to calculate the average age of the members, using the **Average** function. If there were 21 member records, one of which had no entry in the *Date of Birth* field (from which age is found) then the average of the 20 known ages would be calculated. This would be valid, as long as it was recognised as being based on incomplete data. If a count of members was required, basing it on the *Date of Birth* field would give the incorrect result of 20. If you intend to use a numeric field for calculation try to ensure that each record has an entry in that field or that you are careful about how you ask Access to count the records.

Zero length strings

 Nulls indicate that data may exist but is not known. To enter a null leave a field's *Required Property* as 'No' and leave the field blank. A zero length string can be used to indicate that there is no data for the field in that record, for example, a company without a fax machine doesn't have a fax number. To enter a zero length string check that the *Zero length string* property is set to Yes. In the datasheet, type two double quotation marks with no space between, i.e. "". Nulls and zero length strings may be distinguished when searching the data table.

Editing data

Once the records have been entered into a table, this data is available for use, as you will see shortly. It can also be viewed and edited to correct any mistakes. The text and figures within a cell can be edited, deleted or added to exactly as in any other Windows application. The only differences are in how you navigate between the cells and how you select data.

Using Undo

Should you do anything wrong or if something unexpected happens always try **Edit-Undo** or click on the **Undo** button [icon] before doing anything else.

Moving between records

You can move between records in the datasheet using the options on the **Edit-Go To** menu, the *Up Arrow*, *Down Arrow*, *Page Up* and *Page Down* keys or the vertical scroll bar. The most efficient way to move between records in large databases is

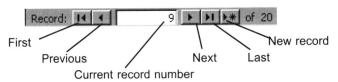

with the navigation buttons in the lower-left corner of the window.

Figure 6.1

Using the navigation buttons

❑ Click on the appropriate button to leap to the first [icon] or last [icon] records in the database, or to move to the next [icon] or previous [icon] ones.

❑ To move to a specific record, click into the record number box (or press *F5*) and type its number then press *Enter*.

❑ Click on **New Record** [icon] to move to the end of the database and start to create a new record.

Selecting data

Various parts of the datasheet can be selected. When an area is selected it appears in inverse colour, so if text is normally black on white, selected text is white on black.

To select	Do This
A single field	Move the pointer to the left-hand side of a cell, so that it changes shape into a white cross, and click.
A word in a field	Double-click on the word
A record	Click in the record selector at the left edge of the record, or click on any field of the desired record and choose **Edit-Select Record**
Several records	Click and drag in the record selector edge for the required number of records.
A column	Click on the heading (the field name at the top of the column).
Several columns	Click on the first column heading required for the selection and drag to the last.

Moving and copying fields

❑ To move data from a field, select it, use **Edit-Cut**, move to the target field and insert it with **Edit-Paste**.

❑ To copy data, select it, use **Edit-Copy**, click in the target cell and use **Edit-Paste**.

❑ If you prefer, you can use these buttons instead of the **Edit** menu options.

Cut   Copy   Paste

Moving and copying records

You can copy a complete table or some records of a table to the clipboard. Records may be moved and copied using **Edit-Cut/Copy** and **Edit-Paste**. You would not normally need to move records within the same table as they can be displayed in any order chosen.

Moving and copying can be carried out between databases providing the table structures are similar. Copying is useful for making a backup of a table. If you decide to revise the data types of fields in a table, it is advisable to make a backup of the table first, in case mistakes are made which could result in the loss of data.

Hiding and showing columns

Columns may be hidden from view. It can be useful to do this where there are a lot of fields in a table, as is the case with the *Membership* table, and you want to be able to see certain columns more clearly. Hiding columns reduces distractions and leaves more screen space for the ones that contain the information you want to see.

To hide a column in a datasheet

1   Click on the column selector at the top of the column. More than one column may be selected for hiding.

2   Choose **Format-Hide-Columns**.

To re-show the columns

1   Choose **Format-Unhide-Columns**.

2   In the dialog box, click in the check boxes to show or hide columns.

3   Click on **Close.**

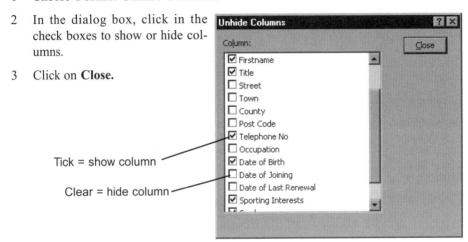

Tick = show column

Clear = hide column

Managing data

What you will learn in this unit

By the end of this unit you will be able to:

❑ use the spell checker

❑ delete data

❑ use find and replace to edit data

❑ print the data in your table.

Managing records

It is very difficult to create a perfect set of data. Mistakes of transcription or keying occur despite data validation techniques and the data itself changes, for example, as members join and leave. Where text fields are used to store descriptions such as occupation or sporting interests then it is useful to be able to spell check the entries.

Deleting records

↔ Old records can be deleted when no longer needed. You can delete a record from a table using a datasheet or a form. (You will meet forms in Unit 13.)

To delete records using a datasheet:

1 Display the datasheet.

2 Select the record or records you wish to delete. Press the *Delete* key (or choose **Edit-Delete** from the menu).

3 Access prompts you to confirm the deletion. Choose **Yes** to delete the record or **No** to restore it.

Finding and replacing

Before you can edit or delete a record, you must first locate it. In a small table, this can be done by glancing through, but in practice databases usually have thousands or even millions of records. The **Find** routine will help you to locate a record.

To find data in a field:

1 Make that field current by clicking in that column.

2 Choose either **Edit-Find...** or click on the **Find** button 🔍 in the toolbar to display the **Find and Replace** dialog box.

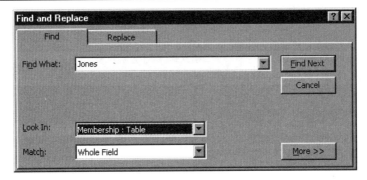

3 Type the characters you wish to find, such as the last name 'Jones', into the **Find What** text box.

4 In the **Look In** box, select either the current field or the whole table.

5 Open the **Match** list and select whether your string should match the whole field, any part of the field or the start of it. A string is a set of characters (letters, digits and punctuation) making up the field data, e.g. a name or a telephone number.

6 Click the **More** button More >> if you want to set the other options.

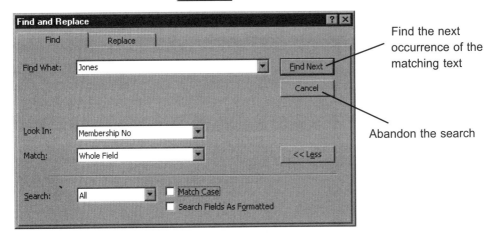

Find the next occurrence of the matching text

Abandon the search

7 In the **Search** box, choose **Up**, **Down** (starting from the current record) or **All**.

8 Tick the **Match Case** option if you want to match the same combination of capital and lower case letters.

9 Tick **Search Fields As Formatted** if you want to match the data as it is formatted, e.g. 14-Jul-01, rather than as it is stored (14/7/01).

10 To start the search click on **Find Next**.

11 When a matching entry is found, its record will be highlighted. If the top or the bottom of the table is reached, you will see a message telling you that Access has finished searching.

12 When you have found the record you want, click on **Close**.

To replace an item of data:

Use this when you need to replace repeated occurrences of an item of data, e.g. when telephone codes are updated.

Follow the steps as for finding, but with these differences.

Start from **Edit-Replace.**

The dialog box has a **Replace With** text box into which you type the text that is to replace the **Find What** text, and two additional buttons.

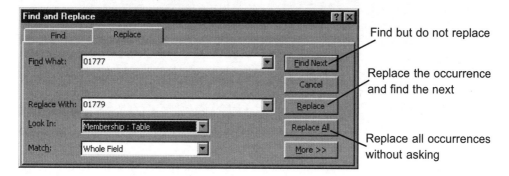

Using the spell checker

With the data displayed in the datasheet, you may spell check a single entry or column(s) selection by clicking on the **Spelling** button . The spell checker will prompt you to correct words that it does not recognise.

Task 1: Editing data

In this task we experiment with finding and replacing data.

1   Open the *Membership* table. Move to the end of the table.

2   Add another record. For the *Category*, enter *3*. Copy the *Lastname* field from record 9 and use **Edit-Paste** to copy it into the *Lastname* field of the new record

3   Finish the record as shown below.

Firstname	Title	Street	Town	County	Post Code
Frances	Miss	70 Meir View	Chelmer	Cheshire	CH2 7BZ

Date of Birth	Date of Joining	Date of last Renewal	Sporting interests	Smoker	Sex
5/5/82	1/3/96	1/3/97	Swimming, judo	No	Female

4   Go to the first record. Click on the *Telephone No* column header.

5   Choose **Edit-Find** or click on the **Find** button in the toolbar.

6   Key *01778* into the **Find What** box and select *Start of Field* in the **Match** box.

7 Click on the **Find Next** button. This should highlight the first occurrence. If the **Find and Replace** dialog box is in the way drag it to the side.

8 Click on **Find Next** to find other matches. Close the **Find and Replace** dialog box.

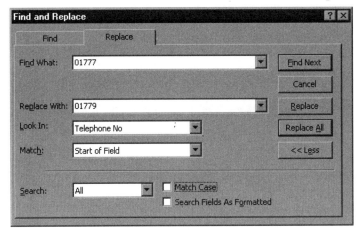

9 Move to the top of the table again and select the *Telephone No* field. Choose **Edit-Replace** and key *01777* into the **Find What** box and *01779* into the **Replace With** box. Limit the search to the current field and select *Start of Field* in the **Match** box.

10 Click on the **Replace All** button.

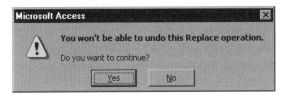

11 Click **Yes** to continue. If you have any doubts about the replacement, click **No** to abandon it.

12 While you cannot *undo* a Replace, you can reverse it by repeating the operation with the Find and Replace strings swapped over. Try it now. Replace all 01779 codes with 01777.

13 Close the **Find and Replace** dialog box.

14 Select the last record, which you have just created, and delete it.

15 Select the *Sporting Interests* column and click the **Spelling** button to spell check it.

Customising the datasheet layout

Adjusting column widths

You can adjust the column widths to make the datasheet display more readable – the default widths tend to be on the large side. Column widths are easily adjusted, especially if you are familiar with Windows applications.

To alter a column width:

1 Move the pointer to the column header.

2 Move the pointer to the dividing line between the column you wish to change and the column to the right, it should change shape to a ↔

3 Click and drag the column to the desired width.

Adjusting row heights

If you make the font larger (see below), you will need to increase the row height to match. If you make the rows deep enough to take two or more lines of text, then long entries will wrap round within cells.

To alter the row height:

1 Move the pointer to the row header.

2 Point to the dividing line between the any two rows – it doesn't matter which, as all rows are adjusted at the same time. The pointer should change shape to a ↕.

3 Click and drag the row to the desired height.

Changing the font used in the datasheet

You can change the font used in the datasheet – but only for the whole sheet, not for selected columns or cells.

1 Choose **Format-Font**.

2 At the **Font** dialog box, set the font, size and other options as desired.

3 Click **OK**.

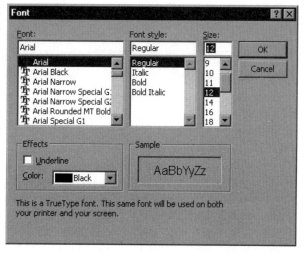

Changing field data types

You may find it necessary to change a field data type as the design of your database develops or if you import data. Before you changes any field data types, make a backup copy of the table in case you accidentally lose data as a result of the changes.

Note the following considerations.

Numeric fields

Changing from one data type to another that can hold a larger number is generally safe, for example from Byte to Integer (refer back to Unit 4 for definitions of field size). If you change to a data type that holds a smaller number, for example from

Double to Integer, then your data will be truncated, in this case by losing the decimal part of the number. Truncation means reducing the number of digits in a number to fit the new field size.

Note: You cannot convert any other numeric type of field into AutoNumber.

Text fields

 The field size of text fields may be altered but if you reduce the size, text may be truncated. Text fields may be converted to Memo fields, but if a Memo field is converted to a text field it will be truncated to 255 characters.

Conversion between data types

It is possible to convert a field from one data type to another, e.g. Text to Number, or Date/Time to Text, but this may result in loss of data.

Primary key or fields used in relationships

You cannot change the data type or field size property of these fields.

To change a field's data type, make a backup copy of your table, display the design view of your table and make the necessary alterations.

Moving columns

You can easily rearrange the order of fields in the datasheet, using 'drag and drop'.

1 Select the column you wish to move.

2 Click again on the column header and drag the column to a new position. A thick vertical line indicates where the field will go when the button is released.

When you close the table you can choose whether or not to make the rearrangement permanent by selecting **Yes** or **No** at the **Save changes** message box.

Displaying data in sorted order

Records are normally displayed in a datasheet in the order in which they were entered. This may not be the order in which you want to see them. You can control the order using the **Sort Ascending** and **Sort Descending** buttons on the toolbar.

To change the displayed order of the records using one field:

1 Click on the field name at the top of the column by which you wish to sort.

2 Click on either the **Sort Ascending** or **Sort Descending** button.

To change the displayed order of the records using more than one field:

1 Arrange the columns so that the ones that you wish to sort by are next to each other, with the highest priority one(s) to the left. Click on the field name at the top of the first and drag across to the last to select the columns.

2 Click on either the **Sort Ascending** or **Sort Descending** button.

Task 2: Customising the membership datasheet columns

1   Display the *Membership* datasheet.

2   Adjust the widths of the columns to accommodate the data displayed.

3   Select the *Sporting Interests* column and drag it to between the *Occupation* and the *Date of Birth* columns.

4   Close the table without making the rearrangement permanent by choosing **No** at the **Save changes** message box when closing the table.

Task 3: Displaying records in sorted order

In this task the records in the *Membership* table will be viewed in different orders.

1   Open the *Membership* table in Datasheet view.

2   Select the *Lastname* column and click on the **Sort Ascending** button. Observe the result. Now click on the **Sort Descending** button and check the new order.

3   Try this for other fields in the table.

4   Select the *Category No* and *Lastname* columns together and click on the **Sort Ascending** button. Note the effect.

5   Drag the *Town* column so it is to the right of the *Category No* column, select these two columns, and click on the **Sort Ascending** button.

6   Drag the *Town* column so it is to the left of the *Category No* column, select these two columns again, and click on the **Sort Ascending** button. Note the difference between these last two sorts.

7   Close the *Membership* table without saving the layout changes.

Printing a table

You can print a table from its datasheet. Access prints a datasheet as it appears on the screen. For large datasheets, Access prints from left to right and then from top to bottom. For example, if your datasheet is three pages wide and two pages long, Access prints the top three pages first, then the bottom three pages. You should preview your datasheet before printing by choosing **File-Print-Preview** or clicking on the **Print Preview** button in the toolbar [image].

If you need to set up your printer, choose the **Setup** button in the **Print** dialog box.

To print a table datasheet:

1   Display the table in Datasheet view.

2   If you only want to print selected records, select them now. To print all the records, select nothing.

3   Choose **File-Print-Preview**, and if the preview is satisfactory choose **File-Print** to display the dialog box.

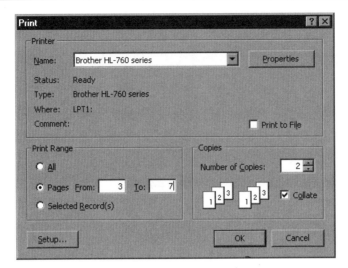

4   Under **Print Range**, choose one of the following:

- **All**, to print all of the records in the table.

- **Pages**, to print specific pages – you should then specify the page numbers of the first and last pages you want to print.

- **Selected Records**, to print a previously selected set of records.

5   Set other **Print** dialog box options if necessary.

6   Click **OK**.

Task 4: Printing the membership table

1   Display the *Membership* table datasheet.

2   Choose **File-Print Preview**, and then select **File-Print...** to display the **Print** dialog box.

3   Under **Print Range**, select **All** and click on **OK**.

4   Close the table.

Reviewing data entry and data management

What you will learn in this unit

This unit reviews and offers further practice on the topics:

❑ entering data

❑ editing data

❑ customising the datasheet

❑ printing a table.

Task 1: Entering and editing data

1 Open the *Chelmer Estates* database then open its *Properties* table.

2 Enter into the *Properties* table the data shown in *Quick Reference 1, Data for tables* (page 127).

3 Use Copy and Paste to duplicate text, where this would be helpful.

Property No	Date of Entry	Selling Price	Address	Town	House Type	N
1	5/6/00	£100,000.00	3, Bude Close	Chelmer	3	
2	20/9/00	£50,000.00	56, Bodmin Drive	Chelmer	3	
3	1/10/00	£111,000.00	187 Dairyground Rd	Chelmer	2	
4	21/10/00	£55,000.00	2, Woodford Rd	Meriton	4	
5	18/11/00	£45,000.00	16, The Close	Branford	3	
6	4/12/00	£87,000.00	67, Steal Rd	Chelmer	3	
7	15/12/00	£89,000.00	258, Chelmer Lane	Meriton	2	
8	2/1/01	£35,000.00	34, Aidelaide Rd	Chelmer	5	
9	5/1/01	£150,000.00	345, Chelmer Lane	Chelmer	3	
10	5/10/00	£200,000.00	16, Park Road	Chelmer	1	
11	12/12/00	£300,000.00	4, The Crescent	Branford	2	
12	2/1/01	£115,000.00	66, Dairyground Rd	Chelmer	2	
13	6/1/01	£80,000.00	15, Pownall Lane	Chelmer	1	
14	3/3/01	£60,000.00	158, Moss Lane	Chelmer	1	
15	15/3/01	£65,000.00	34, The Grove	Chelmer	4	
16	24/3/01	£45,000.00	Flat 1, Gracelands	Woodford	5	
17	26/3/01	£400,000.00	14, Holly Road	Branford	2	
18	5/4/01	£39,000.00	Flat 4, 367 Chelmer Lane	Chelmer	5	
19	9/4/01	£67,000.00	4, St Paul's Avenue	Chelmer	3	
20	26/4/01	£250,000.00	Oaklands, The Crescent	Branford	2	
21	15/5/01	£120,000.00	18, Merrylands Lane	Branford	2	
(AutoNumber)		£0.00		Chelmer	0	

Properties : Table

Record: 14 ◀ 20 ▶ ▶I ▶* of 21

Figure 8.1

Task 2: Customising the datasheet

1 Display the *Properties* datasheet.

2 Adjust the widths of the columns to accommodate the data they contain.

3 Select the *Date of Entry* and *Selling Price* fields and drag them across to between the *Property No* and *Address* fields.

4 Close the table.

Task 3: Printing the Properties table

1 Display the *Properties* table.

2 Select the *Notes* column and click the Spell Check button to check your spelling in this field.

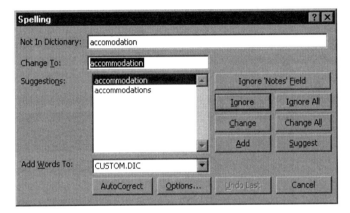

If an error is found, either accept the suggested word (if it is correct) or retype the word in the **Change To** field and click **Change**.

If a word is not recognised, but is correct, either click **Add** to add it to your own dictionary, or click **Ignore**.

3 Preview and print all of the *Properties* table.

4 Close the *Chelmer Estates* database.

Using filters to select records

What you will learn in this unit

Access provides two methods for selecting data, known as filtering and querying. Querying is the most useful method and queries are an integral part of the database. Filtering is less useful but is a quick method that allows you to view a selected set of data. You may therefore omit this unit and move to the next one, which introduces queries. If you do read this unit, you should revisit it after you have completed the units on queries to appreciate the differences of the two methods.

 Filters 'filter out' the records that match specified criteria. They are used in conjunction with tables, queries and forms as a means of displaying selected records, and can be easily switched on or off using the buttons on the toolbar. Trends in data may be identified using filtering. Information concerning, for example, poor membership in a certain category, or property category can easily obtained.

The advantage a filter offers is that it can be designed very quickly while viewing the form, table or query. If records are being amended then it can be useful to select certain records, for example, to change a room for a particular activity.

When a filter is created, it is stored with the table, query or form. Only one filter can be stored but it may be changed if necessary. If you make changes to a filter and do not want to save them, then when you close the table, query or form say *No* to the **Save changes?** question.

By the end of this unit you will be able to:

❑   use a filter to select records using one field as a criterion (Filter by Selection)

❑   use a filter to select records using more than one field as criteria (Filter by Form).

Filter by Selection

A filter created by this method will select records that match the value of the field selected.

1   Select a field displaying a value that is your criterion, e.g. 'Meriton' in the *Town* field, by clicking into the field. Click on the **Filter by Selection** button 🏷.

2   Only the records with that value in the field will be displayed.

↔   To sort the records displayed via the filter use the sorting buttons on the toolbar as described in Unit 7.

3   To remove the filter and redisplay all the records, click the **Remove Filter** button 🏷. This is a toggle switch. Click it again when you want to to reapply the filter.

Task 1: Selecting with a filter

In this task you will filter the *Membership* table to display only those records where the *Town* field is 'Meriton'.

1   Open the *Chelmer Leisure* database.

2   Open the *Membership* table in Datasheet view.

3   Click in a *Town* field that has the value 'Meriton' and click on the **Filter by Selection** button. Only the Meriton records are displayed.

4   Click on the **Remove Filter** button to display all the records. Close the table. You will be asked if you want to save changes. If you do, the filter details are saved and can be used next time the table is opened.

Filter by Form

This takes a little longer to set up, but allows you to create filters records that match the values in more than one field or that match alternative values, for example, 'Meriton' and 'Branford' in the *Town* field.

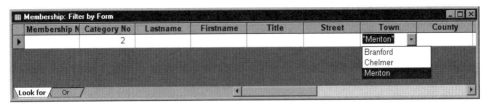

To filter by this method:

1   Click on **Filter by Form** button ▓ on the toolbar. This displays a filter form. The one illustrated below is for the *Membership* table.

2   To specify the criteria for record selection either type the required value into the field, or click on the field, then open and select from its drop-down list. This holds all the different values present in that field in the underlying data.

3   You can specify *And* criteria by setting values in one or more fields, for example, 'Male' in the *Sex* field and '1' in *Category No*.

4   You can specify *Or* criteria using the **Or** tab. This will display another sheet of the form filter. Enter the alternative value here.

↔   The rules of And and Or logic for data selection are the same as for queries and are discussed in Unit 11.

5   Click on the **Apply Filter** button ▽ on the toolbar.

6   To remove the filter click again on the ▽ button (now in its **Remove Filter** mode).

Task 2: Selecting with a filter form

In this task you will use the Membership table and apply a filter to it. Open the *Membership* table in datasheet view. The filter buttons should be in the toolbar.

To select records using a filter form:

1   Click on the **Filter by Form** button to open the Filter Form window.

2   In the *Town* field select 'Branford'. Click on the **Or** tab and select 'Meriton' in the *Town* field.

3   Click on the **Apply Filter** button to display the selected records.

4   To order the records by *Category No* select that field and click on the **Sort Ascending** or **Sort Descending** button.

Editing a filter

A filter created with Filter by Selection will be saved with the form. To change it to use a different field value for selection purposes simply select that field value and click on the **Filter by Selection** button ⬚. If you wish to filter by form instead then click on the **Filter by Form** button ⬚ and specify your criteria.

The same procedure is used to edit a filter that was created using the filter by form technique.

Task 3: Editing a filter

This task follows on from Task 2.

1   Click on the **Filter by Form** button to redisplay the form.

2   Remove the town criteria by deleting them. Set criteria in the *Category No* fields of the two sheets to select categories 3 or 4.

3   Click on the **Apply Filter** button to see the selected records.

4   Experiment with the filter forms, selecting criteria for different fields.

5   Close the table without saving the changes.

Designing a basic query

What you will learn in this unit

The information stored in a database is of no use unless it can be retrieved, and only if it can be retrieved readily and in a meaningful form. Data stored in a telephone directory can be retrieved, for example, by looking up a name in the alphabetically ordered listing, and reading off the adjacent telephone number.

By the end of this unit you will be able to:

❏ question the database by creating a query

❏ display the results in sorted order

❏ sort the resulting dynaset

❏ save a query so that it can be retrieved for later use

❏ print out your query.

Queries play a very important role in database systems. They are used for:

❏ on-line search and retrieval of specific records. For example, to look at a selected set of members for editing, to view the bookings for a given room on a
certain day, or to find the class tutors who have a particular qualification.

❏ creating forms and printing reports. Queries retrieve a selected set of records
and fields; reports are used to print this information. A form based on a query
can be used to restrict data entry to certain fields. Units 13 to 23 introduce
forms and reports.

Queries may be based on more than one table but here all the queries will be based
on the **Membership** table. In more sophisticated databases than our examples, queries may be based on more than one table. This concept is introduced in Unit 24.

The Simple Query Wizard and Query Design window

Creating a query involves two aspects, these are:

❏ selecting the *fields* that are to be shown in the query. It is not usually necessary
to retrieve all fields, for example, the names and telephone numbers may be all
that is needed for a telephone survey of a group of members.

❏ selecting the *records* that are to be shown in the query. For this Access provides a method of querying by which you can describe the characteristics of the
data that you are looking for. This is know as Query By Example (QBE) and is
achieved by allowing you to give examples of the data that you are searching
for in the form of criteria.

Simple Query Wizard

The Simple Query Wizard helps you design a simple 'select' query. A select query will select fields from a table. The Wizard will ask you to select the table you wish to query and which fields you want in your query. It will create the query, which you can then modify later using the Query Design window.

1 At the Database window, click on the **Queries** tab and double-click on **Create query by using Wizard**.

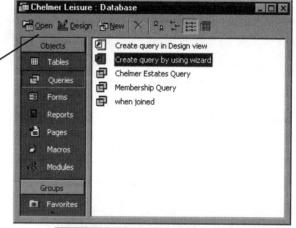

Figure 10.1

If you have not yet created any queries the **Open** and **Design** buttons will not be available

Or Click on the **New** button then select **Simple Query Wizard** in the **Next Query** dialog box and click **OK**.

❑ The **Simple Query Wizard** dialog box will be displayed.

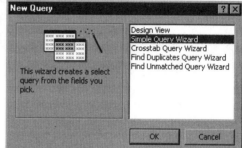

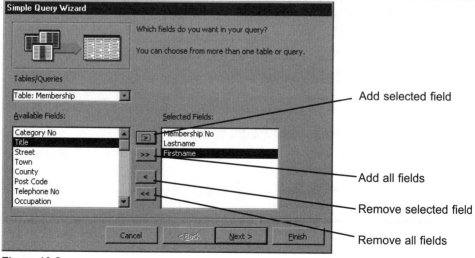

Add selected field

Add all fields

Remove selected field

Remove all fields

Figure 10.2

2   From the **Table/Queries** list, select the table on which the query is to be based.

3   Add fields as required from the **Available Fields:** list to the **Selected Fields:** list.

     To add all the fields to the query, click on the ⏹ >> button.

     To add a selected set of fields, highlight each in turn and click the ⏹ > button.

     If you add fields by mistake, select them and use the ⏹ < button or click the ⏹ << button to remove all fields and start again.

4   When the fields have been chosen click on ⏹ Next > . Give the query a title, select **Open the query to view information**, and click on ⏹ Finish . The result of your query will be shown in Datasheet view.

Task 1: Selecting fields for a query using Simple Query Wizard

1   From the Database window click on the **Queries** tab and double-click on **Create query by using Wizard**.

2   In the **Simple Query Wizard** dialog box, select the *Membership* table from the **Table/Queries** drop-down list.

3   Add the fields *Membership, Firstname, Lastname, Sex* and *Date of joining* to the query by highlighting each field in turn and clicking on the ⏹ > button.

4   Click on ⏹ Next > . Give the query the title ***Dates of joining*** and click on ⏹ Finish . The result of your query will be shown in Datasheet view.

5   View and close the Query window; the name of the query will be listed in the Database window.

Using the Query Design window

The Query Design window (Figure 10.3) allows you to design a query that will select the required fields and records.

Before asking questions of a database you must first decide which tables in the database are required to answer them. The following activities will describe how to ask questions of the *Membership* table. You will see later, in Unit 24 how to include more than one table in a query.

Task 2: Open the Query Design window

1   Click on the **Queries** tab in the Database window and select **Create query in Design view**.

Or Click on the **New** button then select **Design view** in the **Next Query** dialog box and click on **OK.**

2   The **Show Table** dialog box appears in front of the Query Design window. This box allows you to select all the tables needed for the query.

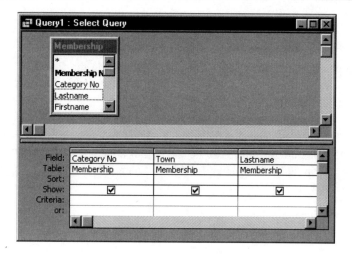

Figure 10.3

3   Select a table and choose **Add** to add it to the query. When the selection of table(s) is complete click on the **Close** button.

This window is in two sections. The upper section holds the windows of the tables used in the query. After choosing the table for the query it will be displayed in its window here, as seen in Figure 10.3.

In the lower section is a grid for the query design. This is where you specify which fields you wish to include in the query and, as you will see later, where you can set query criteria, which allow us to select specific records.

The three most important rows in the grid are **Field**, **Show** and **Criteria**. Each column needs a **Field** name. You can choose as many of the table's fields as you need. The Show box should be ticked if you want the field's data to be displayed in the output. In the **Criteria** row an example of the data may be given and only those records with matching data will then be selected.

As you work your way through this session you will be introduced to the function of the other rows in the grid.

Adding all the fields in the table to the query

The simplest case is where we want to include all the fields in the table.

1   Double-click on the title bar of the field list box of the table in the upper section of the window. This selects all the fields.

2   Click on any of the selected fields (not the *) and drag to the field cell in the lower section of the query window. The pointer should look like a set of record cards.

3   When you release the mouse button all the field names will have been added to the query. Use the horizontal scroll bar to move to the right as all the columns will not fit on the screen.

Adding individual fields in the table to the query

There are three alternative ways of adding the fields one by one to a query.

❑ Double-click on the name of the field required in the field list box in the upper section of the window. It will appear in the next available column in the grid below.

❑ Use the drop-down list associated with each field cell:

1 Click in the field cell in the lower section of the window.

2 A **List box** button appears at the end of the cell. Click on the button and a drop-down list of field names will appear.

3 Click on the name of the field (if necessary scroll through the list) and it will appear in the **Field** cell.

❑ Use the *Drag and Drop* method:

1 Click on the name of the field required in the field list box in the upper section of the window.

2 Drag and drop this field into the field cell in the lower section. While doing this the pointer should look like one record card.

If you drop the field onto a column containing a field, then a column will be inserted to contain the new field.

Removing fields from the query

Fields may be removed singly or in blocks from the query. To remove the all of the fields from the query:

1 Select the first column by clicking on the bar at the top of the column (the pointer will change shape to a down arrow), then drag to select all the columns.

2 Press the *Delete* key or choose **Edit-Delete**.

To remove an individual field from the query, just select the required column for deleting and use **Edit-Delete**.

Viewing or running a query

To see the result of a query, either click on the **Datasheet** button or the **Run Query** button in the toolbar. To return to the query design, click on the **Design** button next to the **Datasheet** button in the toolbar.

Design button   Datasheet button   Run Query button

 Access displays a datasheet containing the records that match the query with fields as defined in the query. This query result is what Access calls a dynaset. A dynaset is a temporary table and is not a permanent part of your database. If you modify your query the resulting dynaset will change accordingly.

Task 3: Selecting fields for a query

In this task you will query the *Membership* table; data from all records will be shown in the dynasets. Initially all fields will be shown and then you will see how to select only certain fields.

1   Starting from the Database window, click on the **Queries** tab.

2   Click on **New** to open a new query and choose **Design view**

3   Select the table *Membership* from the **Show Table** dialog box and close the dialog box.

4   Add all the fields to the query, following the method described above.

5   Click on the **Datasheet** button in the toolbar; you should see the whole of the table forming the dynaset.

6   Click on the **Design** button in the toolbar to return to the Query Design window.

7   Remove all the fields from the query, following the method described above.

8   Add fields individually to the query, experimenting with the different methods described above. Add the fields *Membership No, Lastname, Sex, Date of joining*.

9   Click on the **Datasheet** or **Run Query** button in the toolbar; you should see only these fields from all the records of the table forming the dynaset.

10   Click on the **Design** button in the toolbar to return to the Query design window.

11   By adding and removing fields alter the fields in your query so that they are *Lastname, Sex, Category No, Sporting Interests*.

12   Repeat step 9 to see the output from the modified query.

Sorting the dynaset

The dynaset or result of a query can be displayed in different orders. If no sorting order is specified, the records will be shown in their natural order, i.e. that in which they were entered. Sorting is particularly useful. For example if the records are in date of birth order then it is easier to see an age profile; if records are shown in town order, geographical information becomes apparent. If a report is to be created from the query (see Unit 18) then the order of the records can be defined by the query.

The grid in the lower section of the Query Design window includes a sort row.

To define the type of sorting:

1   Click in the **Sort** cell for the field you wish to sort on.

2   A drop-down list arrow button appears at the end of the cell. Click the button to reveal the sorting choices.

Ascending
Descending
(not sorted)

Ascending will sort from low to high, descending from high to low and not sorted will not apply any sorting.

Note: If more than one field is being sorted, the priority of sorting is determined by the order of the fields in the query; leftmost fields being of higher priority.

Task 4: Sorting

This task investigates the different orders in which the query created in Task 3 can be displayed.

1 From the Design view of this query, click in the **Sort** cell for the *Lastname* field.

2 Open the list box and choose **Ascending**.

3 Display the dynaset by clicking the **Run Query** button. Return to the Design view.

4 Change the sort order of the *Lastname* field to **not sorted**.

5 Choose **Ascending** as the order for the *Sex* field.

6 Display the dynaset then return to the Design view.

7 Choose **Ascending** order for the *Lastname* and **Descending** order for the *Sex* fields. What order do you expect the data for the twins to be shown? View the dynaset.

8 Close the query without saving it.

Saving a query

Sometimes you may wish to ask the same question of a database over and over again, for example, is a membership subscription due? As time passes members need to renew their membership and it is useful to be able to send reminders. A query designed to do this would be saved so that it can be used repeatedly.

To save a query:

1 Choose **File-Save.**

2 In the **Query Name** box of the **Save As** dialog box enter a name that will remind you what the query is about. The name can be up to 255 characters. Click on **OK.**

If you close the query window, you will see the name of your query in the Queries list of the Database window, from where it can be opened for use again later.

Closing and opening a query

To close a query, either:

1 Double-click on the query's control menu button.

Or Choose **File-Close.**

You can open an existing query in either Design view or Datasheet view.

To open a query in Design view:

1 In the Database window, click on the **Queries** tab.

2   Select the query you want to open, and then click on the **Design** button.

To open a query in Datasheet view:

1   In the Database window, click on the **Queries** tab.

2   Select the query you want to open, and then click on the **Open** button.

Task 5: Saving a query

In this task you will save the query created at the end of the previous task.

1   Choose **File-Save.**

2   Give the name *Members' Sporting Interests* to this query and click on **OK.**

3   Close the query and you should see the name of the query in the Database window.

Printing a query

Before printing the dynaset produced by a query it is advisable to preview it first.

To preview a Queries table:

1   Open the query.

2   In the Datasheet view, click on the **Print Preview** button on the toolbar. You will be shown a miniature version of what is to be printed.

3   The pointer becomes a magnifying glass and can be use to zoom in to the page. If you use other Windows applications you will be familiar with this. Click the **Zoom** button 🔍 to toggle between zoom in and zoom out modes. When zoomed in the vertical and horizontal scroll bars can be used to scroll around the preview.

4   Click the right mouse button to get a context menu of preview and print commands.

5   To adjust the column widths you must return to the Datasheet view. To do this, click on the **View** button. The column widths are adjusted in the same way as for table datasheets as described in Unit 7.

Once you are satisfied with the display, you can print from the Print Preview mode.

6   Choose **File-Print.** The **Print** dialog box appears. If you want to print without changing anything *skip the next three steps.*

Note, if you know that the current print settings are what you want, then you can print directly without displaying the **Print** dialog box, by clicking the **Print** button.

7   Click on the **Setup** button and the **Page Setup** dialog box appears.

8   To change the margins, click in the appropriate box and edit the default setting. You can select the orientation of the page, the printer and the paper size. The **Print Headings** check box, if not checked, will suppress the printing of the field names as headings. Click on **OK** to return to the **Print** dialog box.

9   Click on **OK** to print, then click on the **Close** button to return to the query datasheet.

Task 6: Printing

In this task the dynaset produced by the #created in Task 3 will be printed.

1   From the Database window open the query in Datasheet view.

2   Click on the **Print Preview** button on the toolbar.

3   Some columns may need widening. Change to Datasheet view and adjust as required (see 'Customising the datasheet layout', Unit 7).

4   Preview again, zooming in to check the columns widths, then click on the **Print** button.

5   Click on **OK** in the Print dialog box and the following dynaset should be printed.

Surname	Sex	Category No	Sporting Interests
Walker	Male	2	Tennis, squash
Cartwright	Female	1	Aerobics, swimming, running, squash
Perry	Male	6	Judo, karate
Forsythe	Female	2	
Jameson	Female	1	Aerobics, squash
Robinson	Female	3	Swimming, judo
Harris	Male	5	Badminton, cricket
Shangali	Male	2	Weight training, squash
Barrett	Female	1	Keep fit, swimming
Weiner	Male	1	Weight training, squash
Ali	Male	6	Judo, swimming, football
Young	Female	2	Keep fit, aerobics, squash
Gray	Male	5	
Swift	Female	5	
Davies	Female	1	Aerobics, squash, swimming
Robinson	Female	1	Tennis, aerobics
Everett	Male	2	Squash, fitness training, football
Locker	Male	4	
Locker	Female	4	
Jones	Male	1	Weight training

6 Click on the **Close** button to return to the Datasheet view.

Deleting a query

Some queries may only be used once, in which case it is not really worth saving them. Queries that will be used more than once should be saved but a query may have a limited usefulness or be superseded. Therefore, from time to time some queries will need to be removed.

However, care must be taken when removing a query. Later, we will see that reports and forms can be based upon queries so it is important to assign these to alternative queries or to delete them as well. At present there is nothing based on the queries we have created and they may be deleted safely.

To delete a query, from the Database window, click on the **Queries** tab to display the queries. Highlight the query that is to be deleted and press _Delete_.

Task 7: Deleting a query

In this task you will delete the query created using the Simple Query Wizard.

1   Display the queries in the Database window.

2   Select the query, **Dates of joining** and press _Delete_.

3   Reply **Yes** to confirm the delete operation.

Using query criteria

What you will learn in this unit

There are many reasons for asking questions. In business, questions are important in decision making, and to be able to question data relating to, for example, marketing or management, can be very effective using a database management system. In the case of Chelmer Leisure and Recreation Centre the answers to such questions can help with decisions regarding:

❏ where members come from and the effect of local competition

❏ introduction of no-smoking areas and new facilities for older members

❏ discount scheme for loyal members

❏ fees charged for various categories.

To ask questions, criteria need to be set and entered into the criteria cells of the **Query** design grid. Querying is done by example, so an example of the answer to the question is entered into the criteria cell.

By the end of this unit you will be able to:

❏ enter query criteria

❏ rename and hide fields in a query

❏ use logic in queries.

Entering query criteria

Query criteria allow the enquirer to frame questions that enable specific records to be retrieved from the database. We might want to find out various things using the data stored in a table. For example, some questions that might be asked about the *Membership* table are:

❏ Which members live in Chelmer?

❏ Which members smoke?

❏ Which members are over 60?

❏ Which members joined before 1/1/92?

❏ Which members are in categories 1 and 2?

Task 1: Query criteria for the membership table

In this task the questions listed above will be formulated as queries for the *Membership* table. The queries use the data types Text, Number, Date and Yes/No.

Each question will be dealt with in turn.

1   Create a new query using the *Membership* table.

2   Add all the fields to the query.

Which members live in Chelmer?

1   In the **Criteria** cell of the *Town* field type ***Chelmer***.

2   Click on the **Datasheet** or **Run Query** button.

The resulting dynaset should only contain records for which the *Town* field is equal to "Chelmer".

3   Return to Design view. Note that Access puts double quotes around your criterion if it thinks it is text. Delete the criterion "Chelmer" – double-click to select the contents and press *Delete* or click in the cell and use *Backspace* to delete the criterion.

Which members smoke?

1   In the **Criteria** cell of the *Smoker* field type ***Yes***. You may need to scroll to the right to display this cell on the screen.

2   Click the **Datasheet** or **Run Query** button and view the resulting dynaset.

3   Return to Design view. Delete the last criterion.

Which members are over 60?

1   In the **Criteria** cell of the *Date of Birth* field type ***<1/1/41***.

2   Click the **Datasheet** or **Run Query** button and view the resulting dynaset. Return to Design view.

Notice that Access has recognised your query example as a date and has converted it to <#01/01/41#.

3   Delete this criterion.

Which members joined before 1/1/92?

1   In the **Criteria** cell of the *Date of joining* field type ***<1/1/92***.

2   Click the **Datasheet** or **Run Query** button and view the dynaset.

3   Return to Design view. Delete this criterion.

Which members are in categories 1 and 2?

1   In the **Criteria** cell of the *Category No* field type ***<=2***.

2   Click the **Datasheet** or **Run Query** button and view the dynaset.

3   Return to Design view. Close the query without saving it.

Renaming and hiding fields in a query

When queries are printed it is sometimes necessary to widen the column so that the field name at the top can be seen. As this can lead to unnecessarily wide columns, it is useful to be able to rename the field. The field header in a query can be given an alternative name, for example, *Last Renewed* instead of *Date of last Renewal.*

Note: Renaming the field header does not affect the name of the field in the underlying table.

To change field header names:

1 Switch to query design mode by clicking on the **Query Design** button. Move the insertion point to the column containing the field header name you wish to change.

2 Click at the start of the field header. The aim is to put the flashing insertion point at the beginning of the header name. If you accidentally select the header, press *F2* to de-select it. If the insertion point is not at the start, press the *Home* key to move it to the first character position.

3 Type in the new name for the field, followed by a colon – do not put a space before the colon. The colon separates the display name from the field name, which moves to the right to make room for your addition.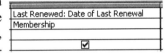

4 Click on the **Datasheet** or **Run Query** button and the query result with amended field header will be displayed.

In the previous unit you saw how to select the fields you want in the result of a query and how to impose criteria. These can be combined so that the dynaset is only of the records that match the criteria and contains only the fields specified in the query. To be able to impose a criterion on a field, that field must be in the query grid, which means that it will normally form part of the dynaset. This may not always be desirable so Access offers the choice of whether or not it should. By default all fields in the query show as the **Show** checkbox is on; to hide a field, click in this checkbox to remove the tick. The field will then not form part of the dynaset.

Task 2: Renaming and hiding fields in a query

Query 1

This query will list the names and addresses of all the male members who smoke.

1 Create a new query using the *Membership* table.

2 Add the following fields: *Membership No, Title, Lastname, Street, Town, County, Post Code, Smoker, Sex.*

3 In the criteria fields of *Smoker* and *Sex* put **Yes.** Hide these fields.

4 Sort the *Lastname* field in ascending order.

5 Rename **Membership No** as *Member No* and display the dynaset.

Member No	Title	Lastname	Street	Town	County	Post Code
13	Mr	Gray	4 The Parade	Chelmer	Cheshire	CH17ER
7	Mr	Harris	55 Coven Road	Chelmer	Cheshire	CH3 8PS
20	Mr	Jones	17 Mayfield Avenue	Chelmer	Cheshire	CH2 90L
1	Mr	Walker	16 Dovecot Close	Chelmer	Cheshire	CH2 6TR

6   Save the query as *Addresses of Male Smokers.* Close the query.

Query 2

In this task you create a query which looks at the occupations of the female members of the centre. The result will be selected fields from selected records.

1   Create a new query using the *Membership* table.

2   Add these fields to the query: *Category No, Firstname, Lastname, Occupation, Sex.*

3   In the **Criteria** cell of the *Sex* field type *No.*

4   Click on the checkbox in the **Show** cell of the *Sex* field to hide it.

5   Click at the beginning of the *Category No* header and type *Cat.* (Remember, no space before the colon).

6   Click on the **Datasheet** or **Run Query** button to view the result of the query. The *Category No* field should have the header **Cat** and the *Sex* field should be hidden.

7   Save the query as *Occupations of Female Members.*

Exploring types of query criteria

The queries that we have created so far have only used criteria in one field. Criteria may be applied to all the fields included in a query. Each field may be sorted or hidden. By combining these facilities, more complex queries can be produced.

We have already used some of the operators used in queries. This table summarises the mathematical operators.

Operator	Meaning
<	less than
>	greater than
<>	not equal to
>=	greater than or equal to
<=	less than or equal to
+	addition
-	subtraction
*	multiplication
/	division

There are a number of **text** operators, of which the most important is the asterisk. "*" can act as a wildcard, standing for any characters. It is used in conjunction with given characters that define part of the text to be selected, for example:

"J*"   text strings beginning with *J*

"*ton"   text strings ending with *ton*

"*k*"   text strings containing the letter *k*

When you use the asterisk in a criterion, the keyword **"Like"** will automatically be added to the start. Like conditions can be set up with quite complex patterns of characters, but apart from the asterisk these are beyond the scope of this book.

Using logic in queries

You can ask questions in queries which relate to more than one field, for example, to find male smokers (Query 1 in Task 2). The question is 'Is the member male AND does he smoke?' There is a logical AND between the two criteria; both criteria must be true for the record to be retrieved.

A logical AND can be used to set several criteria within one field, for example, members whose date of joining was after 1/1/92 AND before 1/1/93 (Query 2 in Task 3 below). In the **Criteria** cell the word 'and' is used between the two criteria, for example, *>1/1/92 and <1/1/93*. More than two criteria may be specified but remember to put the word AND between them.

The other logical operator that is used in queries is OR. An example of this would be a query which requires as its answer the names and addresses of members who live in Chelmer OR Meriton. There is a row entitled **or:** in the query design grid. The way in which this query is set up is to enter *Chelmer* into the **Criteria** row of the *Town* field and underneath in the **or:** row to enter *Meriton*. The example below (Query 3 in Task 3) lists the names of the members who are likely to use the fitness suite as their sporting interests are aerobics, fitness training or weight training.

Task 3: Using different types of query criteria

Query 1 – querying text fields

This query picks out people with particular sporting interests.

1   Create a new query using the *Membership* table.

2   Add the following fields: *Membership No, Lastname, Category No, Sporting Interests*.

3   In the **Criteria** field of *Sporting Interests* type ***Tennis***. Access will convert this to read **like *Tennis***.

4   Sort the *Lastname* field in **Ascending** order.

5   Rename *Membership No* as ***Member No*** and *Category No* as ***Cat.***

6   Display the dynaset.

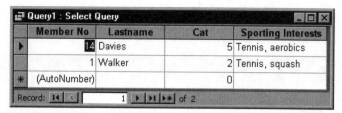

7   Print the dynaset.

8   Save the query giving it the name **Sporting Interest** and close the query.

Query 2 – logic, using AND

This query picks out members who joined in 1992.

1   Create a new query using the *Membership* table.

2   Add the following fields: *Title, Firstname, Lastname, Telephone No, Date of Joining.*

3   In the **Criteria** cell of *Date of joining* type **>=1/1/92 and <1/1/93**. Access will convert this to read >=#01/01/92# And <#01/01/93#.

4   Hide the *Date of joining* field.

5   Sort the *Lastname* field in **Ascending** order.

6   Display the dynaset.

7   Print the dynaset.

8   Save the query giving it the name **When joined** and close the query.

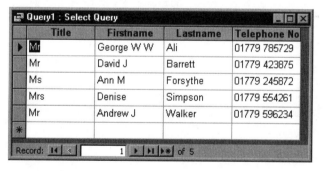

Query 3 – logic using OR

This query picks out members whose sporting interests are aerobics, fitness training or weight training and shows their town so that local interest can be assessed.

1   Create a new query using the *Membership* table.

2   Add the fields: *Membership No, Category No, Lastname, Town, Sporting Interests.*

3   In the **Criteria** cell of *Sporting Interests* type ***aerobics*.** Access will add the word *Like,* whether you type ***aerobics*, '*aerobics*'or "*aerobics*".**

4   In the **or:** cell of *Sporting Interests* type ***fitness training***

5   In the **or:** cell of the row below type ***weight training***

6   Hide the *Sporting Interests* field

7   Sort the *Lastname* field in **Ascending** order

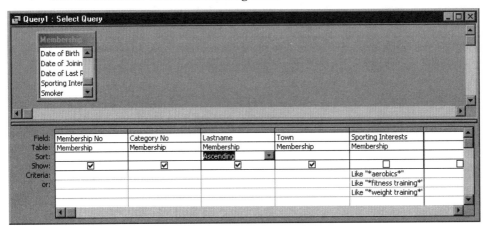

8   Display the dynaset. Notice that when querying text Access is not case sensitive, ***aerobics*** will find aerobics, AEROBICS or Aerobics.

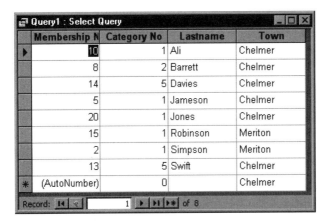

9   Print the dynaset

10   Close the query without saving.

Reviewing sorting and queries

What you will learn in this unit

This unit reviews and offers further practice on queries, using the *Chelmer Estates* database. The following topics are covered:

❏ sorting records

❏ defining the fields to appear in the output from a query

❏ creating queries using basic query criteria

❏ creating queries using logical operators.

Task 1: Sorting the records in a table

This task asks you to experiment with alternative orders for the display of the records.

1   Open the Properties table of the *Chelmer Estates* database in Datasheet view. Sort the records in ascending order of *Selling Price*.

2   Re-sort the records in ascending order according to *House Type*, thereby grouping all properties of a certain type together.

3   Drag the *Selling Price* column next to the *House Type* column so that the *Selling Price* is to the right of the *House Type* column, select both and click on the **Sort Ascending** button. You should see the records in price order within house type.

Task 2: Filtering records

You may omit this task if you omitted the unit on filtering.

1   Open the *Properties* table in Datasheet view.

2   Click on one of the *Town* fields displaying 'Branford'. Click the **Filter by Selection** button to see all the properties in Branford. Click the **Remove Filter** button.

3   Click the **Filter by Form** button. Click the down arrow button of the *Number of Bedrooms* field and select *2*. Repeat for the *Town* field and select *Chelmer*. Click the **Apply Filter** button to view the result.

4   Click the **Filter by Form** button and edit the filter to look for two-bedroomed houses in Meriton as well as Chelmer. Go to the **Or** tab and set the criteria *Meriton* for *Town* and *2* for *Number of Bedrooms*. Click the **Apply Filter** button to view the result. Click the **Remove Filter** button.

5   Close the datasheet. You need not save the changes.

When using OR and multiple criteria you must take care with logic. Here we are looking for two-bedroomed houses in Chelmer OR two-bedroomed houses in Meriton.

If you omit the number of bedrooms criteria in the OR part of the form, all houses in Meriton, irrespective of the number of bedrooms, will be selected. Try it.

Task 3: Defining the fields to appear in a query output

1   Create a series of queries showing all the records in the database, but including only the following fields:

- Property No, Address, Town

- Property No, Town, House Type and Selling Price

- Property No, Address, Notes.

2   Examine each of the dynasets in turn. Try sorting these queries and investigate the difference the field order makes (Unit 7).

3   Do not save these queries. Discuss the circumstances in which each of these lists might be useful.

Task 4: Using basic query criteria

Create a series of queries to answer each of the questions below. Display these fields for records in the dynaset: *Address*, *House Type*, *Selling Price*. Examine the query dynasets. Save each of the queries in turn, using a name of your choice:

1   Which properties are in Chelmer?

2   Which properties are detached houses and also freehold?

3   Which properties have four or more bedrooms?

4   Which properties have a garden that is less than 100 metres in length?

5   Which properties have been in the system since before December 2000?

6   Which properties are detached, have four or more bedrooms and a double garage?

7   Which properties have a granny flat?

8   Which properties have gas central heating?

Why would it be useful to be able to conduct such a wide range of different types of queries on the Chelmer Estates database?

Task 5: Queries using logical query operators

The following queries require the use of the logical operators, AND and OR. Create queries that show all of the fields in the record in answer to these questions:

1   Which properties have a selling price between £80,000 and £100,000?

2   Which properties have either a granny flat or a cloakroom?

3   Which properties have both a granny flat and a cloakroom?

4   Which properties have either a double garage or five or more bedrooms (or both)?

5   Which properties are either bungalows with four or more bedrooms or have a granny flat?

Designing and using screen forms

What you will learn in this unit

In this unit you will learn how to create a screen form. A screen form provides a more user-friendly way with which to work with your data. Entering data can be made easier and less prone to error.

By the end of this unit you will be able to:

❑ create a form using the Form Wizard

❑ save a form

❑ use a form

❑ print a form.

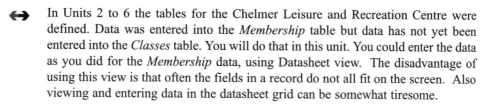 In Units 2 to 6 the tables for the Chelmer Leisure and Recreation Centre were defined. Data was entered into the *Membership* table but data has not yet been entered into the *Classes* table. You will do that in this unit. You could enter the data as you did for the *Membership* data, using Datasheet view. The disadvantage of using this view is that often the fields in a record do not all fit on the screen. Also viewing and entering data in the datasheet grid can be somewhat tiresome.

 When data is collected manually it is often by means of filling out a form. In a form there are boxes to fill in with, for example, name, address, etc. and there may be some that are ticked, such as Yes/No boxes. Access offers the facility to create a form on the screen so that data can be entered into a table by simply filling in the form. If the form has been designed carefully this should be more user-friendly than filling in the cells in a datasheet.

It is usual to have a form for each table of data for the purpose of entering and editing data in that table.

Forms can be used to enter, edit, display and print data contained in your tables. They offer the advantage of presenting data, on screen, in an organised and attractive manner.

Standard forms are created for most applications or jobs, for example, a form for entering the details of a new member, as shown in Figure 13.1.

Access allows you to create forms to your own design, for which it provides a wide range of tools. If you are a new Access user or simply for convenience, the Form Wizard provides a quick and easy way to create a basic form. This basic form can be customised later. To enable us to get started quickly on form design we will make use of the Form Wizard.

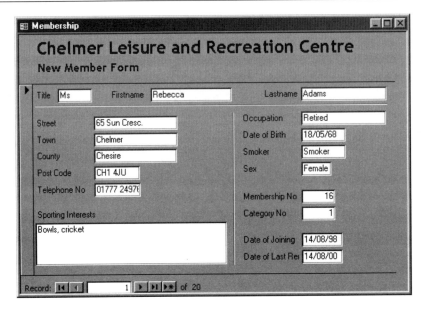

Figure 13.1

We will use the Access Wizards to create a basic form in this unit, which will then be customised in the next unit. There are two kinds of Wizard for creating forms:

1   AutoForm will create a standard form using all fields in the table that you base the form upon.

2   Forms Wizard gives you a little more flexibility over the appearance of your form, and which fields are included.

Creating a form with AutoForm

There are three types of form that can be created using AutoForm: columnar, tabular, and datasheet. A columnar form will display from one record at a time, with boxes for the user to fill in which are arranged in one or two columns. The form shown in Figure 14.1 started as a columnar form but has been modified slightly.

Datasheet forms look like a table in Datasheet view, as you might expect. Tabular forms are similarly laid out, but have boxes instead of a datasheet grid. Both display more than one record at once, so if there are a lot of fields an entire record will not fit on the screen; they are most useful for tables with just a few fields, such as the *Membership* table.

To create a form using AutoForm:

1   Click on the **Forms** button and then click **New** to show the **New Form** dialog box (Figure 13.2).

2   Select one of the AutoForm options.

3   Click on the down arrow of the **Choose the table or query...** box, and select the table or query for which you wish to create a form.

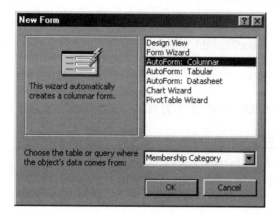

Figure 13.2

4   Click on **OK**.

Autoforms: a word of warning

For most purposes, the Autoform facility is a useful way of creating forms quickly, but in the current version of Access 2000, there seems to be a bug in the way it names forms created with Autoform. At the level of this book, this is not important, but it can be if you go on to create macros. These often need to refer to forms and queries using the object's name, and the bug can then cause problems.

Creating a form using Form Wizard

The Form Wizard will build the same three types of form as Autoform, plus a further type called a justified form. This displays one record at a time in a row format.

To create a form with Form Wizard, click **New** as above, then select Form Wizard and click **OK**. Check that the correct table is listed in the Table/Queries box, and if not, select the right one.

The next stage is to choose which fields are to be on the form. The fields that you can have in the form are shown in the **Available Fields** list.

Transfer these to the **Selected Fields** list by selecting each field and clicking ⎸ > ⎸. You may set the order in which the fields appear on the form by selecting them in the order you desire.

If you wish to *add all* the fields in the table to the form, click ⎸ >> ⎸.

⎸ < ⎸ will remove a highlighted field; ⎸ << ⎸ will remove all the fields from the form.

When you have added the required fields to the form, click ⎸ Next > ⎸. Choose a **Columnar**, **Tabular**, **Datasheet** or **Justified** form.

You are then asked what kind of style you want for your form and are given a choice. An example of the style is shown to the left of the dialog box.

Click on each style in turn to see what it would look like.

Key in an appropriate title for your form into the **Title** box, then click [Finish] to display the form with data in it.

Saving and closing a form

Save a form by choosing **File-Save** or clicking on **Save**.

A form can be closed by **File-Close** or the **Close** button of its window. If the form or the latest changes have not been saved you will be prompted to save. When a form is closed its filename will be shown in the Database window in the Forms area.

To open a form from the Database window, click on the **Forms** button, select the name of the form required and click on the **Open** button.

Task 1: Creating a columnar membership form using AutoForm

In this task you will create a single column membership form, which can later be modified to look like the form shown in Figure 14.1. The order in which the fields are selected for the form is important, as will become apparent when the form is used to enter data. To create this form:

1   From the Database window click on the **Forms** button and click **New**.

2   Display the list of tables in the **New Form** dialog box and select *Membership* from the list of tables. Select **AutoForm: Columnar** and click **OK**.

Access creates a form with a title and a list of paired field names and data in a column. The data showing is from the first record in the table – use the **Record** arrows at the bottom of the window to view or edit other records. Notice that there are some differences between this form and the one shown in Figure 14.1. Customising the form will be considered in Unit 14.

3   Choose **File-Save**, and call the form *Membership*.

4   Close the form.

Creating a tabular form

A tabular form is one that displays several records on the screen at once. The field names are column headings and the records are shown below in a table, rather like in Datasheet view. If there are a lot of fields in a record it is unlikely that you will be able to see the complete record on the screen and you may need to scroll to the right. Tabular forms are best suited to tables with only a few fields, like the *Classes* table. The advantage is that they display more than one record at a time.

A tabular form may be created either using AutoForm or Form Wizard. The following task deals with creating a tabular form using the Form Wizard.

Task 2: Creating the membership category form

No data has yet been entered into the *Classes* table: this task will create a form which can later be used for this purpose.

1   First close any open forms.

2   In the Database window, click the **Forms** button, and then click **New**.

3   In the **New Form** dialog box select the *Classes* table from the drop-down list at the bottom.

4   Select **FormWizard** and click **OK**.

5   Add all the fields to the form and click on the [**Next >**] button.

6   Choose a **Tabular** form with a **Standard** style (click [**Next >**] after each step).

7   Give it the title *Table of Classes*.

8   Click on the [**Finish**] button to display the form. There is no data in this form yet, so there is only one blank record to display. When records have been added, then more than one record is shown in the form, as we shall see later.

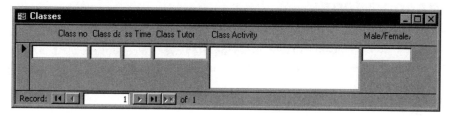

9   Close the form.

Using a form

To use a form, first display the available ones in the Database window by clicking the **Forms** button. To open a form, select it and click **Open**, or double-click on it.

You can use the form to look at the data in the table (or query) upon which it is based. Whether it is a single column or tabular form use the record movement keys in the status bar or the **Edit-GoTo** options to move around the records in your form.

Using the *Page Up* and *Page Down* keys with a single column form will display the next/previous record, whereas with a tabular form they will either page up or down a screen full of records.

Using the form to enter a new record into the table

Forms should be designed with this purpose in mind, as it is their primary function. Entering data is a labour-intensive task and the design of the form is important because a person entering data may use it for long periods.

To enter a new record using a form:

1   Start a new record use the **New Record** button ▶* on the status bar. If your form is
     tabular, click in the first field of the blank record shown at the end of your records.

2   Enter data for the new record by filling in the boxes for each field. When you have
     completed each field, press *[Enter]* or *[Tab]* to move to the next one.

3   Check boxes are used for **Yes/No** fields. Checked is *Yes*, not checked *No*.

Task 3: Using a form to enter data into a table

In this task we shall enter data into the Classes table, using the tabular form.

1   Open the *Classes* form.

2   Enter the data as given in Quick reference 1 (page 127).

↔   As you enter each record it is saved to the *Classes* table.

3   Close the form.

Printing a form

Forms are designed primarily for screen use, i.e. they are intended for data to be
entered and they display it on screen. However, Access offers the facility to print
from a form in case you need to. Remember to preview a form before printing it.

Previewing

Previewing will display a miniature version of what is to be printed. This allows
the layout to be assessed so that adjustments can be made before printing.

To preview a form:

1   Click on the **Print Preview** button in the toolbar, and a miniature version of what is
     to be printed will be displayed.

2   To zoom in and out, just click on the preview, or use the **Zoom** button. Clicking on
     the right mouse button will allow you to select the degree of magnification.

3   Choose **File-Page Setup** to make adjustments such as the orientation of the paper
     (portrait or landscape), the choice of printer and width of margins. Click **OK** when
     the required adjustments have been made.

Printing

When you're happy with the layout, you can print from the preview or the form
screen.

1   Choose **File-Print**.

2   Select whether all pages of the form will be printed or just selected ones, and specify
     the number of copies. Click **OK**.

Task 4: Printing the Classes form

1 Open the *Classes* form.

2 Click on the **Print Preview** button.

3 Experiment with zooming in and out.

4. Use **File-Page Setup** and/or **File-Print** to make adjustments to the paper and printer setup before printing. If no adjustments are necessary, then click **Print**.

5. Close the form.

Customising forms

What you will learn in this unit

Forms are constructed from a collection of individual design elements, which are called controls. If you are familiar with Windows applications you will be familiar with dialog boxes and the controls that they contain. The controls that appear on the forms created so far are:

- ❏ labels, so that you know what each part of the form is for

- ❏ text boxes, for entering data.

↔ There are other controls, which will be introduced in Unit 21.

By the end of this unit you will be able to:

- ❏ display the customising tools (toolbox, palette, properties and field list)

- ❏ move and size controls

- ❏ align controls

- ❏ add text to a form

- ❏ add the date

- ❏ add headers and footers to a printed form.

Customising a form

A form may be modified so that it is easier for inexperienced users to enter information into the database. To modify a form you need to display the form in design mode (see the following section). AutoForm or Form Wizard is a good way of quickly creating a form. However, the resulting form is rather standardised in terms of vertical spacing between controls, fonts and colours, so you are likely to wish to make modifications.

Components of a form in Design view

Component	Description
Form header	Typically contains text such as the form's title, but may also hold field headers and graphics.
Detail	Contains the controls (field labels, text boxes and check boxes) that display data from the underlying table.
Form footer	Used like the header, typically holding the date and similar items.

Right margin	The position of the right margin is indicated by a vertical line on the right edge of the form. It can be moved by clicking and dragging.
Bottom margin	A horizontal line that indicates the bottom margin of the form. This also can be positioned by clicking and dragging.
Scroll bars	Vertical and horizontal scroll bars enable movement of the form within its window.

If you have used a Form Wizard to create the form, only the detail band and possibly the header band contain controls. The header band contains information, which will always appear at the top of the form, usually the title. The detail band contains the controls for displaying the data.

Form Design view

So far a form has only been opened in 'form run' or Data view. This is the mode in which forms are usually run where they display and more importantly, accept data. A form can also be shown in Design view, where its layout and appearance can be modified. Data cannot be entered in this view.

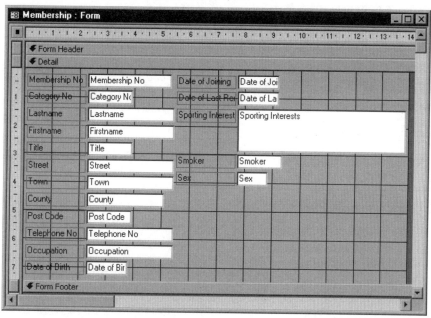

Figure 14.1 Membership form in Design view

Label and text box controls

A field usually has two controls: a label control in which the field name appears and a text box control in which the data will appear when the form is run.

The field names are shown in the controls instead of the data, as in Data view. The labels and controls may be moved, resized or reformatted to produce the desired layout and appearance.

Design aids

Other features of Design view are:

❑   rulers and grid

❑   design aids in the form of other small windows:

❖   the Toolbox

❖   the Field List

❖   the Properties Sheet.

The **Toolbox** offers a selection of tools with which controls and text may be added to the form.

The **Field List** shows a list of fields in the table on which the form was based.

The Properties Sheet is a list of properties. The properties will depend upon what part of the form is selected.

You will become familiar with these as you progress through the tasks. To display these windows click on the buttons:

▤   the Toolbox   ✖   the Field List   ▥   the Properties Sheet

Or use the commands, **View-Toolbox**, **View-Field List** and **View-Properties**.

Colour selection

Colour selection can be made using the drop-down buttons on the Formatting toolbar.
↔   These will be considered in Unit 22.

Opening a form in design view

To open a form in Design view, from the Database window:

1   Click on the **Forms** tab.

2   Select the name of the form required and click on the **Design** button.

Once a form is open you may switch between form run (Data) view and Design view by clicking on the button on the toolbar, or by selecting **View-Design-View**, or **View-Form-View**.

▦ ▾   Form View   ▨ ▾   Design view

Moving and sizing controls

Before you can move or size a control you must select it. A control is selected by clicking anywhere on it. When selected, the control is enclosed by an outlining rectangle with an anchor block at its upper left corner and five smaller blocks. The smaller blocks are sizing handles. On columnar forms, text boxes often have associated labels and when you select one of these they are selected together as a unit.

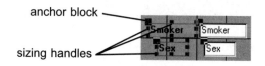

anchor block

Figure 14.2   sizing handles

To...	Do this
Select a text box and its label (if it has one)	Click anywhere on either the label or the text box.
Move a text box and its label (if it has one)	After selecting, move the pointer over the label until it changes shape to a hand. Click and drag the text box to its new position.
Move label or text box separately	After selecting, move the pointer over the anchor block at the top left corner of the label or text box. The pointer should change shape to a pointing hand. Click and drag to new position.
Adjust the width and height together	Move the pointer over a sizing handle at one of the three other corners (i.e. not the top left). It should change to a diagonal two-headed arrow. Click and drag to size required.
Adjust only the height of the control	Move the pointer over a sizing handle in the middle of the top or bottom of the outline. It should change shape to a vertical two-headed arrow. Click and drag to height required.
Adjust only the width of the control	Move the pointer over a sizing handle in the middle of the left or right-hand side of the outline. It should change shape to a horizontal two-headed arrow. Click and drag to width required.

Selecting and moving a group of controls

You can select and move more than one object at a time. This is useful if you want to keep the relative spacing of a group of objects while you move them to another part of the form.

To select a group of objects, either:

❑ imagine a rectangle that would touch or enclosed the objects; use the pointer and click and drag to draw this rectangle on the form; when you release the mouse button all the objects covered by this rectangle will be selected, or

❑ select one object, hold down the *Shift* key and select the next and subsequent objects.

To move:

❑ *the whole group*, with pointer as the shape of a hand, drag

❑ *an individual control in the group*, point to its anchor handle and drag.

To deselect:

❑ *the whole group*, click anywhere outside the selected area

❑ *one object in the group*, hold down the *Shift* key click on the object.

Using the ruler and the grid

The **View-Ruler** command will select whether or not the ruler is displayed. When a control is being dragged, indicator lines slide along both rulers to aid positioning of controls.

View-Grid will display or hide a grid, which is also an aid to the positioning of controls. The spacing of the grid can be adjusted by adjusting the setting of the **GridX** and **GridY** properties on the form's property sheet. To display the form property sheet use **Edit-Select Form** and click on the **Properties** button.

When **Format-Snap to Grid** is on (indicated by a tick by **Snap to Grid** in the menu), any new controls drawn on the form will have their corners aligned to points on the grid. When **Snap to Grid** is off, the control can be placed anywhere.

Aligning a group of controls

Once you start to move controls around the form they can become untidy as they become misaligned. By selecting a group of controls together they can be aligned. Select labels and text boxes separately for alignment purposes.

To align labels:

1 Select the labels by clicking on each label while holding down the *Shift* key, or draw a rectangle that encloses part or all of all the labels you wish to select.

2 Choose **Format-Align** and as these are labels select **Right**. The selected group of controls should all align to the right.

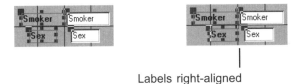

Figure 14.3   Labels right-aligned

To align text box controls:

1 Select the text box controls by clicking on each text box while holding down the *Shift* key.

2 Choose **Format-Align** and as these are text boxes select **Left**. The selected group of controls should all align to the left.

Figure 14.4   Text boxes left-aligned

Changing the form's area

The area of each section of a form – the header, detail and footer – may be altered individually. Also, the position of the right and bottom edge of a form may be adjusted.

To alter the depth of a section of the form:

1   Move the pointer to the bottom edge of the section, where it will change shape.

2   Drag down to increase the depth of the section.

To alter the area of the form drag the right and bottom edges to the required size.

Task 1: Customising the membership form

The aim of this task is to create the form shown in Figure 14.1. We don't give exact instructions as you can experiment with selecting and moving controls. You may find it useful to widen the form so that controls can be moved to temporary positions while you rearrange them, then shrink the form back to the required size when you have finished.

If you wish to keep a group of controls together, select them as a group and then they can be moved as *a* group. Also try aligning groups of controls to achieve a tidy looking form.

1   Open the *Membership* form in Design view.

2   If you inadvertently delete a field from the form see the following table for instructions on how to restore it.

3   When you have rearranged the detail section save the form design using **File-Save**.

Deleting or restoring form fields

To...	*Do this*
Delete a label and text box	Select the control and press *Delete* or use **Edit-Delete** to delete both label and entry box.
Delete only the label	Click on the control then on the label before deleting.
⚠	*If you delete a field you won't be able to use the form to enter data into this field. Use **Edit-Undo** immediately if you accidentally delete one.*
Restore a label and field	Use **View-Field List** to display the list of fields in the table. Click on the field name required and drag into position on the form. If the form is a single column form then both label and field will appear, although the label will require editing. If the form is tabular then just the field will be restored.

Changing the text of a field name label

The text of a field name label may be edited and, if required, additional text can be added to the form.

To...	Do this
Add a label	Click on the **Label** tool in the **Toolbox** , click on the form in the required position and type the text.
Edit a label	Double-click on the label to display an insertion point in the text. Edit the text as required. Press *Enter* or click on a blank part of the form when finished.

Altering the size and font of controls

To alter the size or font of controls in a form:

1 Select the control(s) to be altered.

2 Open the **Font** list box in the toolbar and select the font required.

3 Open the **Point Size** list box and select the point size required.

4 Click on the **Left**, **Centre** or **Right** alignment button on the toolbar.

If you increase the size of a font you may need to alter the size of the control and the size of the section.

Task 2: Adding text to the form header

In this task you will add text to the header section of the *Membership* form.

1 Open the *Membership* form in Design view.

2 Widen the form header section.

3 Click on the **Label** tool in the Toolbox window.

4 Click in the space created for the form header and key in the text ***Chelmer Leisure and Recreation Centre.***

5 Increase the size of the label and text. You may wish to change the font.

6 Move and size the heading as in Figure 14.5, and add the text ***Membership Application Form.*** If you wish you may alter the font or size of this text.

7 Save and close the form.

Task 3: Using the customised form to enter data

To gain a full appreciation of the modifications made to the *Membership* form then it should be used to enter data.

1 Open the form from the Database window by clicking on the **Open** button.

Figure 14.5

2   Move through the records and display a blank form.

3   Compose data for a new member and using the form, enter data into the next record.

4   Close the form.

Reorganising the field order

When data is entered into each field, _Enter_ or _Tab_ takes you to the next. The order in which the fields are entered is defined by the order in which they were selected in the Wizard. If the layout has been modified, this order may need to be changed.

To change the tab order of the fields:

1   From Design view, choose **View-Tab Order** to display the **Tab Order** dialog box (Figure 14.6). This displays the order of the fields in the **Custom Order** box. In the **Section** box the Detail section is normally selected.

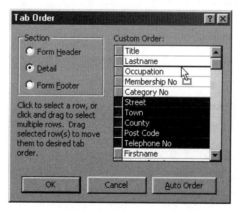

Figure 14.6

2   To alter the order, select the field(s) to be moved and drag to the new position.

3   When the new order has been selected click on **OK**.

The **Auto Order** button will set the tab order according to the way in which the fields are laid out on the form, working left to right and then top to bottom.

Adding headers and footers

Headers and footers are always displayed on the screen. It is straightforward to add text into these, and simple enough to add calculated text, such as the date.

If a form is to be printed, the header section prints before the first record and the footer prints after the last. Extra sections – *page header* and *page footer* – can be added which will print on each page. You can control whether to display or print these. Calculated text may be added to show the page numbers.

Page breaks may occur in the middle of records, if the record is in single column format. This can be avoided by adjusting the **Keep together** setting of the **Detail** properties from **No** to **Yes** (see Figure 14.7).

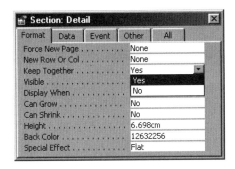

Figure 14.7

To display the Properties sheet check that the **Properties** button is depressed and click on the **Detail** bar.

Task 4: Adding the date

The aim of this task is to put the date in the *Table of Classes* form footer.

1 Open the *Table of Classes* form in Design view.

2 Choose **Insert-Date and Time**. Select a suitable date format and click on **OK.** The date and time will be inserted into the header.

3 Cut and paste to move the date and time into the footer.

4 Switch to run mode by clicking on the **View** button to see the result.

5 Close the form.

Task 5: Adding headers and footers to a printed form

When a form is printed the header is printed at the beginning and the footer is printed at the end of the records. To add a header and footer at the top and bottom of each page of the *Membership* form when printed:

1 Open the *Membership* form.

2 Click on the **Print Preview** button.

3 Close the preview and display the form in Design view.

4   Choose **View-Page Header/Footer**. Two extra sections appear, **Page Header** and **Page Footer.**

5   Select all the title in the form header and use **Edit-Copy** (you need to select the label, not the text within the label).

6   Click on the Page Header bar and use **Edit-Paste.** Position the pasted copy.

7   Click on the Page Footer bar and choose **Insert-Page-Number**. Choose a suitable format and click on **OK.**

8   Click on the Form Header bar. To display the **Properties** sheet, click on the **Properties** button on the toolbar.

9   In the **Section FormHeader** properties box select the **Format** tab.

10   Click in the **Display When** box to open the list and select **Screen Only.**

11   Click on the Detail bar and change the **Keep Together** property to **Yes** to prevent page breaks in the middle of records.

12   Preview and print the form.

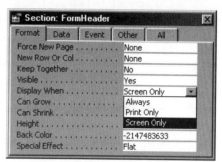

Reviewing forms

What you will learn in this unit

This unit reviews and offers practice on the following topics:

❑ creating and saving forms

❑ using forms

❑ printing forms

❑ customising forms.

Task 1: Creating forms

1 Use the Form Wizard to create a form for entering data into the *Chelmer Estates Properties* table. Since we will normally enter records as new properties are registered with the estate agency, a single column form, which presents a form for entering one record at a time is the most appropriate. Try creating a form similar to the one shown below.

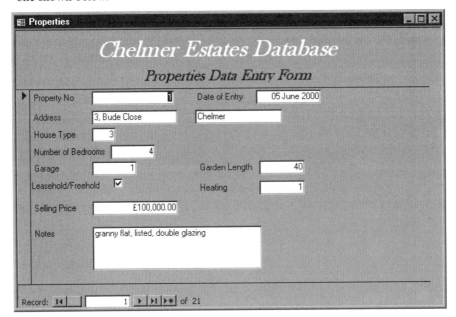

Figure 15.1

2 Save the form as *Properties.*

Task 2: Using a form

Remember that when a blank form is displayed (ready to accept data for a new record), default values will have already been entered for those fields for which you set default values when you were defining the field properties in the table definition process.

1   Enter two records of your own choice into the **Properties** table using the form **Properties...**

2   Experiment with entering data that contravenes the validation rules and check that these are operating appropriately.

3   You may leave these additional records in the table.

Task 3: Printing from a form

1   Preview the form on screen in order to see how it will look when printed.

2   Print one page of the form.

↔   Remember that forms are intended for screen use, and that if you routinely wish to print a set of records you should use a report (see Unit 16). Printing of forms is most useful for examining screen design.

Reports

What you will learn in this unit

This unit explores the basic design of printed reports that include data from an Access table. It explains how to create a report quickly using Report Wizard. Later units develop some of these themes more fully.

By the end of this unit you will be able to:

❏ create a report using Report Wizard or AutoReport

❏ save and close a report

❏ use a report to print data from an Access table.

Printing information from a database

Reports are used to print information from a number of records, which can come from a table or a query. Reports may also show summary information relating to the records displayed. Graphs created with Microsoft Graph may also be added.

Reports allow you to select the data to be printed and then to present that data in an acceptable format. Unlike forms, reports are intended to be printed. Forms are normally displayed on screen, though they can be printed if required.

In most applications you will create a number of different standard reports. For example, a mailing list of clients may simply show customer name and address, but a list of outstanding orders to specific clients will also show details of the items customers have ordered, their value and other associated information.

Access give you a wide range of tools with which you can create reports from scratch, but it is quicker and easier to use the Report Wizard. This will give you a basic report which you can later format and customise. We use Report Wizards here because they allow you to understand the basic concept of what a report is and how it works, before you grapple with customising specific features of the report.

Since forms and reports share many design and creation features, you will re-use some of the skills that you acquired earlier in designing a form.

Creating a single-column report with Report Wizard

There are various types of report that can be created with Report Wizard. First we deal with the single-column report, which is used most frequently and is relatively simple to create. A single-column report places all the selected fields in a single column, with their field names to the left.

1   To enter Report wizard starting from the Database window, either click on **New** in the Database window when you are displaying reports, or click the **New Object** button on the toolbar and select **Report**. A **New Report** dialog box appears (Figure 16.1).

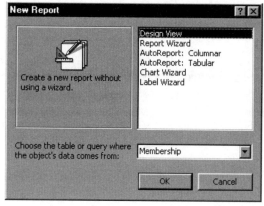

Figure 16.1

2   Select the **Report Wizard** option to create a report using Report Wizard.

3   Click on the down arrow of the **Choose the table or query...** list box, to produce a list of tables and queries and select the table for which you wish to create a report.

4   Click on **OK**.

5   The next stage is to choose which fields are to be in the report. The possible fields are shown in the **Available fields** box (Figure 16.2).

6   These can be transferred to the report by selecting each field in turn and clicking on the > button.

7   If you wish to add all the fields in the table to the report, click on the >> button.

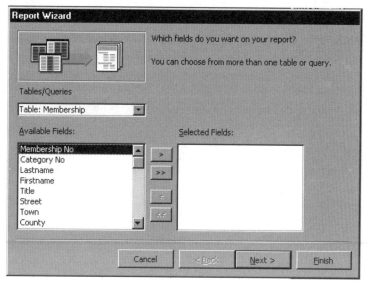

Figure 16.2

8   You may set the order in which the fields appear on the report by selecting them in the order that you desire. The `<` button will remove a highlighted field and `<<` will remove all the fields from the report.

9   Once you have added the required fields to the report continue by clicking on the `Next >` button.

10   The next dialog box asks you to indicate grouping levels. Leave this for now and click on the `Next >` button. We shall return to this in Unit 17.

11   The next step asks you to select the sort order. Select the fields you want the records to be sorted by. If you have only a small set of records, a single sort field will be adequate. If you want records to appear in the same order as in the table or query, it is not necessary to indicate a sort field. Click the `Next >` button.

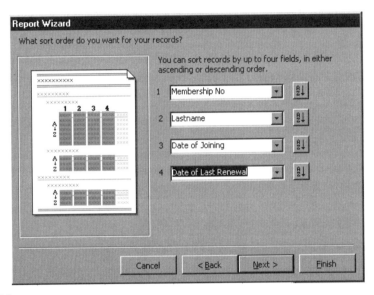

Figure 16.3

12   The next step relates to the report's layout and orientation (portrait or landscape). The choice of layout depends on whether or not grouping is used. On the first occasion, if a grouping is used, choose **Outline 1** and **Portrait**. If no grouping is used choose **Columnar** and **Portrait**. Click on `Next >`.

13   You are then asked what kind of style you want for your report. You are given a choice of:

❑   Bold

❑   Casual

❑   Compact

❑   Corporate

❑   Formal

❑   Soft Gray.

14 The style determines the appearance of the field names and field contents in the report. An example of the style is shown on the left of the dialog box. Click on each style in turn to see what it would look like. On the first occasion a report is created choose **Corporate**. The style can be modified later. Click on the Next > button.

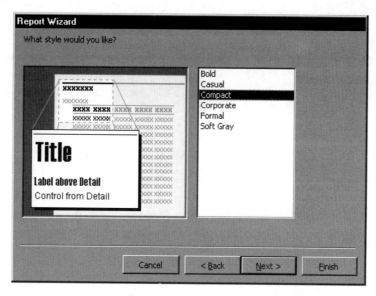

Figure 16.4

15 You are next asked for a title. Report titles are particularly important in flagging the purpose of the report to the reader, so type in something that conveys a clear idea of its contents.

16 Select the **Preview the report** option and click on Finish. Note that Access has added a page number and the date at the bottom of every page.

Saving and closing a report

Save a report by choosing **File-Save**. If this is a new report that does not have a name, Access will prompt for a file name with a **File-Save As** dialog box. If you later want to save a report under another name use **File-Save As**, and enter the new name in the dialog box.

 Remember that there is a distinction between the name and the title of a report. The title is the text that is displayed at the top of the report when it is printed. The name you give when saving the form is the form's file name, which you need to be able to recognise when you want to open the form for use again. These names appear in the Database window when the **Report** tab is selected.

Task 1: Creating a vertical (single-column) report using Report Wizard

We wish to create a single-column report, which lists all the members in the database, showing the following fields.

- ❏ Membership No
- ❏ Category No
- ❏ Firstname
- ❏ Lastname
- ❏ Occupation
- ❏ Date of Birth
- ❏ Sporting Interests.

We want the report to look like the following extract.

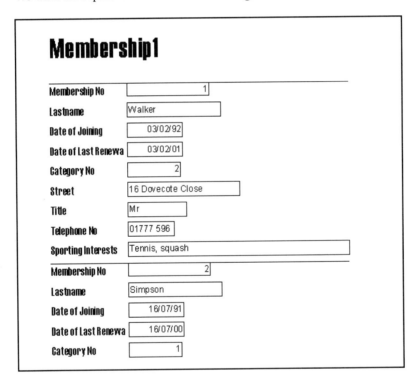

Figure 16.5

1   To enter Report Wizard starting from the Database window, go to **Reports** then select **Create report by using wizard** or click on the **New Object** button on the toolbar and select **Report**. At the **New Report** dialog box select the **Report Wizard** option.

2   Click on the down arrow button of the **Choose table or query...** list box, to produce a list of tables and queries, and select the *Membership* table. Click on **OK.**

3   Select the fields to appear in the report by clicking on the field names above in the **Available Fields** list box, and then clicking on the ▸ button. The selected fields should appear in the **Selected Fields** list box. If you include any fields by mistake, use ◂ to remove them. Click on Next > .

4   Do not indicate a grouping level; if Access has automatically created one (on *Category No*) then click on ◂ to remove the grouping. Click the Next > button.

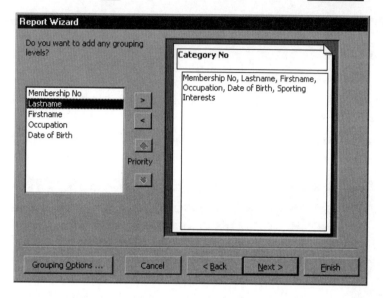

Figure 16.6

6   Choose to sort by *Membership No* by entering it in the first box. Click on Next > .

7   Choose **Columnar** and **Portrait** for the report layout.

8   Choose **Corporate** for the **Style** of the report. Click on Next > .

9   Enter the following report title: ***Chelmer Leisure and Recreation Centre Members***

10   With the option **Preview the report** selected, click on Finish to display the report on the screen.

11   Access will save the report with the name *Chelmer Leisure and Recreation Centre Members*, the same as the title.

Using a report

To use a report, first display the available report names in the Database window, then double-click on the report name. The Print Preview window will appear showing a preview of how the report will appear when printed. Alternatively, click on the report name and then click on the **Preview** button.

To zoom in and out and to view a complete page on the screen, click on the report.

Note that a report picks up the properties of the table or query used when it was designed. Later, you change the properties of the table or query without changing the properties of the report.

Printing a report

Before printing any report always view the report in Print Preview.

Previewing

To preview a report:

1 Click the **Preview** button, and a miniature version of what is to be printed will be displayed.

2 To zoom-in and zoom-out click anywhere on the preview, or use the **Zoom** button. Click on the **Zoom Control** box to select a specific magnification for the preview.

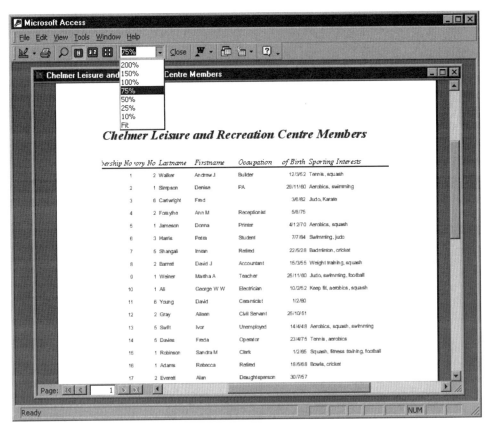

Figure 16.7

3   Choose **File-Page Setup** to make adjustments such as the orientation (portrait or landscape), the choice of printer and the width of the margins. Some of the options in the **Page Setup** dialog box will be familiar since you will have used them in printing tables and queries, but there are also special options for use when printing report, such as the number of items (records) across the page, item size, and item layout. Click on **OK** when the required adjustments have been made.

Printing

When satisfied that the preview is correct, printing may be done from either the preview screen or the design screen.

To print from the preview screen:

1   Click on the **Print** button in the Print Preview bar.

To print from the design screen:

1   Choose **File-Print.**

2   Select whether all or certain pages of the report will be printed and the number of copies. Click on **OK**.

Task 2: Using and printing a report

To use the report *Chelmer Leisure and Recreation Centre Members*, first select it from the file names displayed in the Database window, by double-clicking on the report name. The Print Preview window will appear showing a preview of how the report will appear when printed.

To print the report:

1   Choose **File-Page Setup**. Experiment with the Setup options. Close the **Page Setup** dialog box between each trial in order to view the new layout in **Print Preview.**

❏   Set two columns to the page by selecting the **Columns** tab and entering *2* in the **Number of Columns** box. You may need to adjust the **Width** in the **Column Size** section to less than half your page width.

❏   With two columns, explore the effect of **Down, then Across** and **Across, then Down** in the **Column Layout** section.

❏   Increase the column **Height.**

2   When you are happy with the layout, print it, by selecting the **Print** button.

Creating a report using AutoReport

The really easy way to create a report is to let Access to do all the work, with AutoReport. This, however, does not give you any scope for specifying the contents or style of the report.

Task 3: Creating a tabular report using AutoReport

This task demonstrates how easy it is to create a report using AutoReport.

1   Click on **Reports** and **New**.

2   In the **New Report** dialog box select either **AutoReport: Columnar** or **AutoReport: Tabular.**

3   Click on the down arrow button of the **Choose a table or query...** list box, to open the list of tables and queries and select the table for which you wish to create a report – in this case, the *Classes* table.

4   Click on **OK** and the report will be created and displayed on the screen in preview mode.

5   Use **File-Save** to save the report as *Classes* and print it.

Grouped reports

What you will learn in this unit

This unit explores creating reports where records are arranged in groups according to the value of fields in a table or query.

By the end of this unit you will be able to:

❑ create a report with grouped records.

Note: You may choose to omit this unit for the moment and return to it later when you are ready to design this kind of report.

Understanding grouped reports

A grouped report places its fields in a row and groups the records according to the values in one or more selected fields. This approach can also be used simply to create a report in a table form with fields shown in columns, if you do not specify groups. The advantage of this type of report is that it displays more records to the page. However, is does not display records with several long fields, which therefore cannot be accommodated next to each other on the page in parallel columns.

Records can be grouped by several different fields, although we shall use only one field for grouping.

Apart from the need to define how records will be displayed in groups, the process of creating a groups/totals report is similar to that for a single-column report. The process is basically:

1 Select the fields to appear in the report.

2 Select how the records in the table or query will be grouped for the report. Groups are divisions that include all records that have a value for a specific field.

3 Select the order in which you want the groups created (if you are using more than one group).

4 Select how the records are to be sorted for the report.

5 Select a layout.

6 Select a style.

7 Add the report's title.

8 Use Print Preview to display the report on screen.

9 Save the report.

10 Print the report, as appropriate, and subsequently, close it.

Task 1: Creating a grouped report using Report Wizard

We wish to create a grouped report that lists all the members for which there are records in the database, showing the following fields:

❏ Category No

❏ Lastname

❏ Firstname

❏ Telephone No.

The records are to be grouped by *Category No*, i.e. all records with a given *Category No* are shown together. We wish to create a report, which looks like this.

Membership2

Category No Lastname	Firstname	Telephone No
1 Adams	Rebecca	01777 24976
1 Ali	George W W	01777 78572
1 Jameson	Donna	01777 63756
1 Jones	Edward R	01777 54872
1 Robinson	Sandra M	01777 85426
1 Simpson	Denise	01777 55426
1 Weiner	Martha A	01777 87452
2 Barrett	David J	01777 42387
2 Everett	Alan	01777 34875
2 Forsythe	Ann M	01777 24587
2 Gray	Aileen	01778 12384
2 Walker	Andrew J	01777 59623
3 Harris	Petra	01778 58713
4 Locker	Alison	01777 64287

Figure 17.1

1 At the Database window, go to **Reports** then select **Create report by using wizard** or click on the **New Object** button on the toolbar and select **Report**. At the **New Report** dialog box select the **Report Wizard** option.

2 From the **Choose the table or query...** drop-down list box select the *Membership* table. Click on **OK**.

3 Select the fields to appear in the report by clicking on their names in the **Available Fields** list, then clicking on the [>] button. The selected fields should appear in the **Selected Fields** list. If any fields are included by mistake, click on them in the **Selected Fields** list and click [<] to remove them. Click on [Next >].

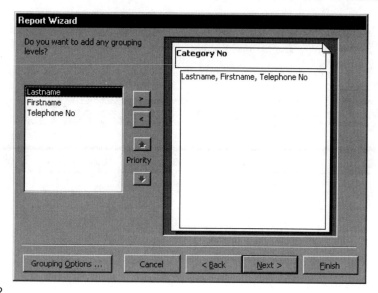

Figure 17.2

4   You may find that Access has automatically grouped the records by *Category No*. If not, select *Category No* in the list of fields then click on [>] to display it in the heading box in the preview. Click [Next >].

5   Sort records within groups alphabetically by the *Lastname* field. Click [Next >].

6   Select **Stepped** and **Portrait** for the layout of the report. Click [Next >].

7   Select Compact for the style of the report. Click [Next >].

8   Enter the report title: *Members by Membership Category*.

9   Choose **Preview the report** and click [Finish]. As the wizard has created the report it is saved with the name of its title i.e. *Members by Membership Category*.

10   To print the report directly, click on the **Print** button.

11   To change print options display the **Print** dialog box using **File-Print** and make the choices you require before clicking on **OK**.

Task 2: Creating a grouped report using more than one group

In this task you will create a grouped report which lists all the members for which there are records in the database, showing the following fields:

❏ Category No

❏ Lastname

❏ Firstname

❏ Town

❏ Telephone No.

The records are to be grouped according to *Category No* and *Town*, so that, all records with a given *Category No* are grouped together and within this grouping all records with a given *Town* will be grouped together.

We wish to create a report, which looks like the one shown below.

Members by Membership Category and Town

Category No	Town	Lastname	Firstname	Telephone No
1				
	Chelmer			
		Adams	Rebecca	01779 249761
		Ali	George W W	01779 785729
		Jameson	Donna	01779 637564
		Jones	Edward R	01779 548721
	Meriton			
		Robinson	Sandra M	01779 854267
		Simpson	Denise	01779 554261
		Weiner	Martha A	01779 874521
2				
	Branford			
		Gray	Aileen	01778 123845
	Chelmer			
		Barrett	David J	01779 423875
		Everett	Alan	01779 348751
		Forsythe	Ann M	01779 245872
		Walker	Andrew J	01779 596234

Figure 17.3

1 Follow the first four steps as for the previous task. If Access has not automatically grouped the records by *Category No*, click on *Category No* in the list of fields and then click on [>] to display it in the heading box in the preview.

2 To add *Town* to the grouping select it and click on [>]. Click [Next >].

3 Sort records within groups alphabetically by the *Lastname* field. Click [Next >].

4 Select **Stepped** and **Portrait** for the layout of the report. Click [Next >].

5 Select **Compact** for the style of the report. Click [Next >].

6 Enter the following report title: *Members by Membership Category and Town.*

7 Choose **Preview the report** and click [Finish]. The report will be saved with the name of its title i.e. *Members by Membership Category and Town.*

8   To print the report directly, click on the **Print** button.

9   To change print options display the **Print** dialog box using **File-Print** and make the choices you require before clicking on **OK**.

Task 3: Selecting the order of grouping

1   Create a report that is the same as the one in Task 2, with the records grouped according to **Category No** and **Town.** This time show all records with a given **Town** grouped together and within this grouping show all records with a given **Category No** grouped together.

2   Create this report as in Task 2, and when you have added **Town** as a grouping, click on the **Priority** up arrow to change the priority of grouping.

3   Continue as before but title this report *Members by Town and Membership Category.* Note the difference between this report and the previous one.

Mailing label reports

What you will learn in this unit

Mailing label reports allow the creation of mailing labels, from, say, a table of names and addresses. A mailing label report fits its fields into a rectangle designed to print labels. Unlike other Report Wizard reports, this type does not show field names. It does, however, make it easy to add text such as commas and spaces.

By the end of this unit you will be able to:

❏ create a mailing label report

❏ use a query as the basis for a Report Wizard report.

Creating a mailing label report

The procedure for creating a mailing label report is similar to that for creating any other type of report, except that you use a special Label Wizard.

To create a mailing label report:

1 With **Report** displayed in the Database window, select **New.**

2 Click on the **Label Wizard** option and select a table or query to provide the data for the labels report. Click on **OK** to start the Label Wizard (Figure 18.1).

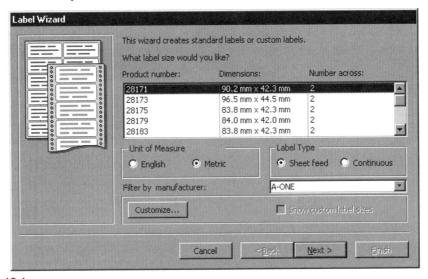

Figure 18.1

3   Select the size of labels from the list. Label sizes are listed according to their Avery number. If you do not know the Avery number for a given label size, look at the **Dimensions** and **Number Across** columns to find the size that matches your labels.

4   Select **Unit of Measure** and **Label Type** and click on Next >.

5   Select the **Font name**, **Font size**, **Font weight** and **Text color**. You may also check **Italic** and/or **Underline** (Figure 18.2). Click on Next >.

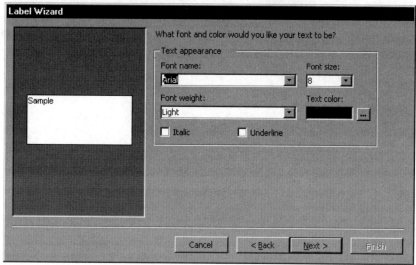

Figure 18.2

6   Select fields as with other report types, so that they appear on the prototype label but remembering that more than one field can be added to a line.

7   Add text, fields and punctuation as required (Figure 18.3). To advance to a new line, press *Enter*. When you have created the label, click on Next >.

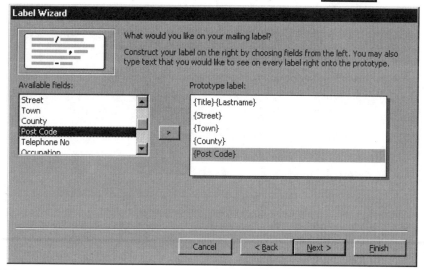

Figure 18.3

8   Select how the records are to be sorted, i.e. the order in which mailing labels are to be printed (Figure 18.4). Click on ⬚ Next > ⬚ .

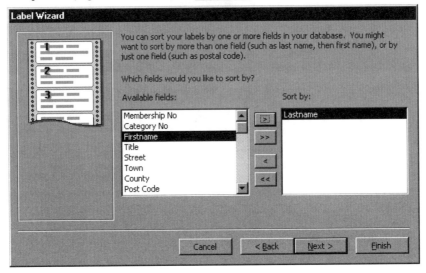

Figure 18.4

9   Either accept the suggested name or type in a different name for the report. With **See the mailing labels as they will look printed** selected click on **Finish** to display labels on screen.

10 Save the report.

11 Print and close the report as appropriate.

Task 1: Creating a mailing label report wizard report based on a query

We wish to create a mailing label report, which lists all members who have joined since 1/1/99. An extract from such a report is shown below. First we need to define and execute a query to select the appropriate records, and then we need to define the mailing label report that is to be used to display this set of records.

Mr Harris	Mrs Barrett
55 Coven Rd	7 Oldcott Way
Chelmer	Meriton
Cheshire, CH3 8PS	Cheshire, CH9 3DR

Query design and execution were introduced earlier, and you may wish to review this topic at this point.

To define the query:

1   Starting from the Database window, click on the **Queries** tab, and click on the **New** button to create a new query.

2   Select **Design view** and click on **OK**.

3   The **Show Table** dialog box appears. Select the table *Membership* and click on the **Add** button, then click on the **Close** button.

4   Include all fields in the query by double-clicking on the title bar of the **Field List** box of the table in the upper section of the window. Click anywhere in the selected area and drag to the field row to transfer all the fields to the lower section.

5   In the *Date of Joining* criteria cell enter the query criteria *>1/1/99*. To view the result of this query click on the **Run** button on the toolbar.

6   Save the query by choosing **File-Save**.

7   At the **Save As** dialog box, enter the **Query Name** *New Members*.

8   Close the query.

To design a report to display the records retrieved by the query:

1   Click on the **Reports** tab in the Database window and click on **New**.

2   Select the **Label Wizard** option to create a report using Label Wizard.

3   From the **Choose a table or query...** drop-down list select the query *New Members*. Click on **OK**.

4   Select the size of the labels. You may need to experiment with different label sizes. Try metric Avery number L7160 first. Click on [Next >].

5   Leave the font as default and click on [Next >].

6   Select the fields to be included. These are, in the order that follows.

     ❏   Title
     ❏   Lastname
     ❏   Street
     ❏   Town
     ❏   County
     ❏   Post Code

7   Add the field *Title* followed by a space and then the field *Lastname* to the first line. Click on the *Enter* key to move onto the next line.

8   Add *Street* to the next line.

9   Add the remainder of the fields, each on a separate line, with the exception of *County* and *Post Code*, which should be on the same line separated by a space. Click on [Next >].

10   Choose to order the records in alphabetical order according to **Lastname**.

11   Accept the title **Labels New Members**. The report is automatically saved.

12   With **See the labels...** selected, click on [Finish] to display the report on the screen.

13   To print the report directly select the **Print** button.

14   To display the Print dialog box use **File-Print**.

Customising a report

What you will learn in this unit

This unit explores some of the basic tools for designing customised reports instead of using the standard reports that can be created using Report Wizards.

By the end of this unit you will be able to:

❑ appreciate the component parts of a report

❑ create a blank report as a basis for later design work

❑ move and size controls

❑ change the report's area

❑ delete, add and restore fields to a report

❑ change the text of a field name

❑ add headers and footers.

Understanding customised reports

Although Report Wizard produces a useful basic report, eventually you may wish to create your own from scratch, so that you can exercise greater control over the design. If you examine the Report Wizard reports that you have created recently you will note that they have these limitations: the title length is restricted; the spacing is fixed; horizontal spacing that makes it difficult to distinguish between records; and the fixed format gives the same standard appearance time and time again.

This unit explores some of the simple tools for customising a report. These may be applied either to a report created initially with Report Wizards, or to create your own report. Before attempting to create or modify a report it is useful to identify the components of a report. These are listed and described below. If you examine the reports that you have just created using Report Wizards, you should recognise that they have these components. If you display an existing report in Design view, by clicking on the **Design** button with the report selected in the Database window, the report will be displayed with these areas clearly marked.

Components of a report

Component	Description
Report header	Contains any headings or other introductory text that might appear at the beginning of the report.

Page header	Contains headings that will appear at the top of each page, such as a running title and page numbers.
Detail	Shows data from the records in the database. Sets up the format for records in general which is then used for every record included in the report.
Page footer	Appears at the bottom of each page.
Report footer	Contains information at the end of the report, such as a final summary or a statement such as 'This is the end of the report'.
Group header	Marks the beginning of a group; usually contains the group name.
Group footer	Marks the end of a group and often contains sections that summarise the records that are part of a group.

Working with report design allows you to adjust the content, size and position of everything that appears on the report. As with forms, each item of a report is called a *control*. Controls include a field's data, text, picture and calculations. Many of the features relating to forms that you experimented with earlier also apply to reports.

Modifying an existing report

To customise an existing report it must be selected in Design view.

1   Select the report in the Database window and then click on the **Design** button

Or

2   Right-click on the report name and choose **Design** from the shortcut menu.

Creating a new blank report

To create a new report, without the aid of Report Wizard:

1   Open the **Reports** tab in the Database window and click on **New**.

Or

Choose **View-Database Objects-Reports** and then click on the **New** button in the Database window.

Or

Click on the down arrow of the **New Object** button and select **Report**.

3   Select the **Design view** option to create a report without using Report Wizard.

4   Click the down arrow button of the **Choose the table or query...** box to open the list of tables and queries and select the one for which you wish to create a report.

5   Click on **OK**.

Design aids

When you create a new blank report the Toolbox window will be displayed. This is useful for adding controls to the report. There are a number of such windows, which you will encounter as you advance in report design. These are listed below.

Window	Description
Properties sheet	Tto change different features of the report's contents
Field list	To add controls bound to fields
Toolbox	Contains the design tools (can be dragged to left of screen where it locks as a toolbar)

All of these windows can be moved or closed in the same way as any other window. They can also be opened and closed from the **View** menu.

Task 1: Examining the components of a report

1   Examine one of the reports that you have created with Report Wizards in Unit 18.

2   With the Database window displayed, click the **Reports** tab, then the **Design** button. Note that Report Wizards create reports with default settings in many areas.

3   Examine the report that you have displayed. Click on each control in turn. What are the default settings for the following?

❏   Report Header

❏   Page Header

❏   Detail

❏   Page Footer

❏   Group Header

❏   Group Footer

❏   Report Footer

Task 2: Creating a blank report

Create a blank report for the *Classes* table, showing all of the fields in the table.

1   Click on the **Reports** tab in the Database window, and then the **New** button. Select the *Classes* table from the **Choose the table or query...** drop-down list.

2   Select the **Design view** option. Click on **OK.**

3   Consider the layout and decide where to put title, field labels and the fields themselves.

4   Add all the fields to the report from the field list. Display the field list; double-click on the field list title bar to highlight all the fields.

5   Click and drag the highlighted fields onto the **Detail** section of the report. Controls for all the fields should appear.

6   Save as *Classes* and close.

Moving and sizing controls

Moving and sizing controls is the basic activity for improving the appearance of the report.

In order to move a control, it must first be selected. It can then be moved by dragging. The different types of controls can be selected in the same way as they are selected and moved on forms. If you need a reminder, see 'Moving and sizing controls' in Unit 14.

Task 3: Moving and sizing controls on an existing Report Wizards report

We wish to improve on the design of the report **Chelmer Leisure and Recreation Centre Members,** so that the final report looks like this.

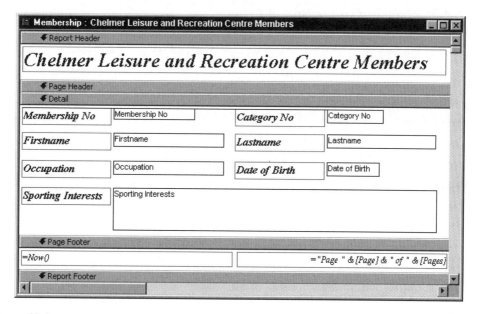

Figure 19.1

1 First open the existing report. Select the report **Chelmer Leisure and Recreation Centre Members** in the Database window and then select the **Design** button.

2 Move the controls on the report until it resembles the design screen shown above, using the instructions above for selecting and moving controls. If the toolbox is in the way, remove it by using **View-Toolbar**.

You may get into a muddle in your first attempt to move controls. Remember that controls can be deleted by selecting them and using the _Delete_ key. If all else fails, close without saving and start again.

3 View the new report on screen using **Print Preview**.

4 Save the report as *Members2* using **File-Save As**.

Customising a report

Changing the report's area

The areas in each section of a report – the header, detail and footer, may be altered individually. It is also possible to adjust the position of the right and bottom edge of a form.

To alter the depth of a section of the form:

1 Move the pointer to the bottom edge of the section, where it will change shape. Drag the pointer to a new location.

2 To alter the area of the report, drag the right and bottom edges to the size required.

Deleting, adding and restoring fields

When you create a report from scratch it is necessary to add appropriate fields from a selected table or query. You may also wish to add or delete fields when changing an existing report. Procedures are similar to those for deleting, adding and restoring fields to or from a form.

Changing the text of a field name label

The text of a field name label may be edited and if required additional text can be added to the form. Again, procedures are similar to those for forms.

Task 4: Creating a customised report

We wish to open the report that we created earlier, *Classes*, add fields and modify field labels, in order to create a report like the one shown below.

Chelmer Leisure and Recreation Centre: Sports, Fitness and Exercise Classes

Classes

Number:		1	Class Tutor:	Evans
Class Day	Monday		Class Activity:	Ladies' Aerobics
Class Time		10:00	Male/Female/Mixed:	Female
Number:		2	Class Tutor:	Franks
Class Day	Monday		Class Activity:	Weight Training
Class Time		11:00	Male/Female/Mixed:	Male

Figure 19.2

1 First open the report called **Classes** by selecting the **Reports** tab in the Database window, and then selecting the **Design** button.

2 Click on the fields and their labels and move them into a more satisfactory position. Rearrange them as necessary.

3   If you inadvertently delete a field, display the **Field List** window and drag the field onto the report.

4   Edit the field label *Class No* so that it reads ***Number***. Select the field label control, click where the text editing is required and modify its name. Modify other labels as necessary in the same way.

5   Press *Enter* or click on another part of the report to complete changes.

6   Try aligning groups of controls to achieve a tidy looking form. Select a group then use the options on the **Format-Align** submenu.

7   Create a report header and a report footer by choosing **View-Report Header/Footer** so that a tick is placed beside this option.

8   Create a text box control. Click on the **Label** tool Aa in the Toolbox then place the pointer in the **Report Header** area and drag to create a box large enough to accommodate text.

9   Type the following text into the report header band: ***Chelmer Leisure and Recreation Centre – Sports, Fitness and Exercise Classes.***

10   Repeat these steps to insert text in the report footer, page header and page footer.

11   Print preview the report, save it as ***Classes*** and close it.

You have now created a report showing all of the basic information, but clearly there is much scope for improvements to its format. A few of these are explored in the last tasks in this unit, but the majority are the subject of the next few units.

Reformatting a report

Altering the size and font of controls

To alter the size or font of text on a report:

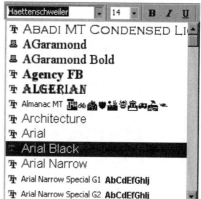

1   Select the controls to be altered.

2   Click on the **Font** list box in the toolbar and select the font required.

3   Click on the **Font Size** list box and select the point size required.

If you increase the size of a font you may need to alter the size of the control and the size of the section.

Adding headers and footers

Page headers and footers can be easily added to a report. With the toolbox displayed click on the **Label** tool. Place the pointer in the appropriate header or footer box and drag it to make a box large enough to accommodate the text.

Task 5: Reformatting a report

This task reformats the report created in the last task using some of the additional features that have been introduced above.

1   Open the report called *Classes* in Design view.

2   Select the controls in the **Report Header**, open the **Font Size** list box and select an appropriate larger point size. Click on the **Bold** button to make the text bold. Click on the **Centre** button to centre the text within the control. If necessary, stretch the control box to display all of the text.

3   Move the field labels into the page header band by first selecting them as a group. Choose **Edit-Cut** and click anywhere in the page header. Then choose **Edit-Paste**.

4   Rearrange the labels in the page header to make column headings. Select these as a group and format them, making them bold, italic and slightly larger.

5   Adjust the size of the page header so that it just accommodates the labels by dragging the bottom of the page header.

6   In the Detail area, rearrange the controls to align with the labels in the page header. If necessary expand the boxes to accommodate the longest field value. For example make sure that the control box for **Activity** accommodates "Badminton".

7   In turn, select the text boxes for *Class No* and *Time* and left justify them by clicking on the **Left Align** button. Select the **Male/Female/Mixed** control box and delete it by pressing the *Delete* key.

8   Select and format the report footer in italics.

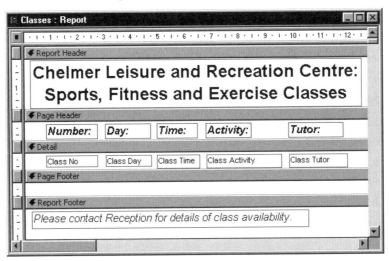

Figure 19.3

9   Move back and forth between Print Preview and Design view as often as necessary, making changes and viewing their results, until you are happy with the appearance of your report.

10   Print preview, save as ***Classes2,*** close and print as required.

Chelmer Leisure and Recreation Centre: Sports, Fitness and Exercise Classes

Number:	Day:	Time:	Activity:	Tutor:
1	Monday	10:00	Ladies' Aerobics	Evans
2	Monday	11:00	Weight Training	Franks
3	Monday	15:00	Body Conditioning	Latham
4	Monday	19:00	Step Aerobics	Wheildon
5	Tuesday	10:00	Men's Multi-gym	Jackson
6	Tuesday	14:00	Ladies' Multi-gym	Evans
7	Tuesday	19:00	Family Multi-gym	Jackson

Figure 19.4

Tools

The report design window has a number of tools that you have used in designing a report. It is useful to review these briefly.

❑ The **Ruler** measures the distance from the top and left corner of the report. It can be removed or replaced by choosing **View-Ruler**.

❑ The **Grid** appears in Design view. Access automatically aligns controls with the grid. It can be moved or replaced by choosing **View-Grid**. To deactivate the grid choose **Format-Snap to Grid** and clear the tick.

❑ The **Align** option. Use **Format-Align** to align selected controls relative to each other.

Consolidating report design

Use the following tasks to practise the report creation skills you have gained from this and the last three units.

Task 6: Creating a single-column report using Report Wizard

Produce a report, based on the *Membership* table, which lists these details for all members who are smokers.

❑ Membership No
❑ Category No
❑ Title
❑ Firstname
❑ Lastname
❑ Occupation
❑ Date of Birth
❑ Sex.

1   First define a query, which selects the records for the members who are smokers.

2   Save this query and use it in the design of a report using Report Wizards. Don't forget to save the report, as *Smokers*, and preview it on screen before printing.

Task 7: Creating a groups/totals report using Report Wizard

You wish to create a report that lists all the classes offered by the centre, based on the *Classes* table. The report is to be organised in groups according to *Class Activity*. All fields in the *Classes* table are to be included.

1   Produce a second groups/totals report, based on the *Classes* table, which details all the information in the *Classes* table.

2   Sort the report in classes order.

3   Save this report as *Classes List*.

Task 8: Creating a customised report

Instead of using Report Wizard to create the report in Task 6, attempt to create the same report independently of the Report Wizards tool, i.e. as a customised report.

Adding lines and rectangles

What you will learn in this unit

This unit is the first of a series that deal with techniques to change the appearance of the information on a report or form, and to make their presentation more exciting. Access offers a wide range of tools for formatting forms and reports and supports the imaginative creation of interesting designs. Forms and reports created using Wizards use some of these features to a limited extent, but by the time you have completed these units you should be able to improve on Wizard designs.

By the end of this unit you will be able to:

❑   add lines and boxes to forms and reports.

Understanding design

Although the tools we explore in these units allow you to be very adventurous with your designs, remember that in good design, less is often more. Be sparing in your use of coloured boxes and lines, and don't go wild with fifty different fonts! A few tips to bear in mind are listed below, but before you start, ask yourself a couple of questions:

❑   Are you designing a form or a report? Forms will be used on-screen, whereas reports are likely to be printed out on paper to be read once or occasionally referred to. This has implications for layout, font sizes and colours.

❑   Who will be reading/using it? Data entry personnel may have to use your forms for long periods at a time, so be functional, use toned-down colours with clear but not harsh contrast between text and backgrounds. Reports for presentations on the other hand need to be eye-catching, with plenty of space around the important bits, and may carry the organisation's colours and branding.

Design tips

❑   Keep forms simple and easy to read. Don't use unnecessary text and graphics, and try to ensure that the whole form fits onto a normal screen comfortably to avoid scrolling where possible.

❑   Use colour sparingly – if there are logically distinct sections of a form, it may be helpful to mark them off somehow, but don't let colour become a distraction.

❑   Think of how the form will be used and place controls in sensible places – for instance, if a user is entering membership data from a paper form filled in by a new member, make sure that the fields on the form appear in the same order so that you can work through it easily.

❏ Maintain a consistent appearance for related forms. This looks more professional and makes it easier for a user to get used to a series of forms.

❏ Design reports with your printer in mind. Is it colour or black and white? Do
   large pictures slow it down unacceptably? Can it handle fine detail or subtle
   colour graduations?

❏ What is the purpose of the report? Focus on the particular piece of information
   which is important. If you have a lot of information on one report, but different
   bits are relevant to different people, split it into smaller reports targeted to
   specific audiences.

Adding lines and rectangles to forms and reports

Lines and rectangles can be added to emphasise portions of the form or report or to
separate one part from another. Here you'll learn how to add plain lines and rectangles – colours and special effects are dealt with in Unit 22.

To add a line:

1   Select the **Line** tool in the **Toolbox**.

2   Point to where you want the line to start.

3   Click and drag the pointer to where the line should end, and release the mouse
    button.

To add a rectangle:

1   Select the **Rectangle** tool in the **Toolbox**.

2   Point to where you want one corner of the rectangle to be.

3   Drag the pointer to where the opposite corner should be, and release the mouse
    button.

To delete a line or rectangle, just select it and press _Delete_. To move or resize one,
select it and click and drag on the edges as you would for any other control.

Changing layer order

When you add lines and rectangles to a form or report, imagine that they are drawn
on a transparent sheet (called a 'layer') which is placed over the top of any features
already on the screen. You'll see if you try overlapping a line or rectangle with a
control that the control is partially obscured by it. Rectangles have a transparent fill
by default, but when you add coloured fills to rectangles in Unit 22, you'll find that
controls underneath it seem to disappear altogether!

To remedy this, you'll need to change the order of the layers so that the controls sit
on top of the rectangle or line, not underneath it.

1   To move a control back beneath other controls, select it and choose **Send to Back**
    from the **Format** menu.

2   To move a control from behind other controls and put it on top, choose **Bring to Front** from the **Format** menu.

Note: if you are having difficulty selecting a control which is "stuck" behind another one, select a nearby control and use the *Tab* key to hop from one control to the next until you have the hidden one selected.

Task 1: Adding lines and rectangles

Open the **Classes** form. Experiment with adding lines and rectangles to the form until it looks similar to the form shown below.

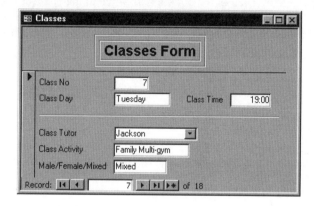

Figure 20.1

1   Move and size the controls so that they are in the positions shown above.

2   Edit the text of the labels appropriately.

3   Place two rectangles around the text in the form header.

4   Insert a line underneath the controls for Day and Time.

5   Save the form as *Classes3*.

Style enhancements

What you will learn in this unit

Style enhancements include alignment, colour, 3-D effects, fonts and borders. These properties are listed in the bottom half of the property sheet window and may also be set using buttons on the toolbar. When a control is selected that can or does use any of these style enhancements, the toolbar buttons shown below become active.

By the end of this unit you will be able to:

❑ use different alignments

❑ use different fonts

❑ set dimensions

❑ set colours

❑ set borders.

Setting alignment and fonts

This activity uses the toolbar to set font style, size and text alignment. Select a control, then click on an appropriate icon on the toolbar to apply the style.

Button	Action
Font	
`Arial ▼`	sets the font style of characters
`8 ▼`	sets the font size of the characters
B	sets characters in bold type
I	sets characters in italics
U	underlines characters
Alignment	
≡	left aligns text
≡	centres text
≡	right aligns text

These buttons work in much the same way as Microsoft Word, so if you are familiar with that program, you'll be at home here. The main difference is that to apply a style, you have to select the *control*, not the *text* on the control – you'll find that when you have the text itself selected for editing, the style buttons are inactive. The other difference is in the way alignment works: alignment refers to the text's position inside the control box, *not* the control box's position on the screen.

For those of you not familiar with formatting text in MS Word, a 'font' is a style of lettering; this style can be further modified by changing the font size (measured in 'points'), or applying bold (heavy print), italics (slanting letters) or underline (you work it out!). Experiment with different fonts, sizes and styles until you have a good feel for how they work – but remember not to go font- and style-crazy when producing a final design. You should also bear in mind that not all printers and not all computers will necessarily have the same fonts available as you, so for professional purposes, stick to common ones such as Arial, Comic Sans, Courier New, the Lucida family of fonts, Times New Roman and Verdana. If in doubt, have a look on a couple of other computers and see which fonts are common to all.

When printing reports, try to use True Type fonts only – these are designed so that they print out exactly as they appear on he screen. True Type fonts have a symbol like this next to them in the **Font Name** menu: ⊤.

The alignment buttons determine where the text sits inside the control box:

❑   left align means that the text starts at the left-hand edge of the control box

❑   right align means that it ends flush with the right-hand edge

❑   centre align places it right in the middle.

 These alignment buttons should not be confused with the **Align-Left/Right/Top/Bottom** options available when you right-click on a group of selected controls – those set the position of the controls on the page relative to each other, whereas these buttons affect the text inside the control boxes.

Task 1: Setting alignment and fonts on forms

Open the *Classes3* form. Set the alignment and fonts as shown in Figure 21.1.

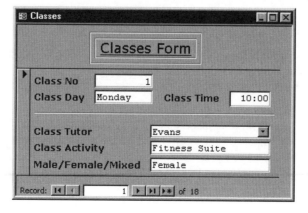

Figure 21.1

1   Change the font of *Class No*, *Class Day* and *Class Time* to Verdana, make them Bold, and set the field controls to Courier New.

2   Increase the font size of all of them to 10 point. You may need to increase the size of the controls to accommodate the text of the labels and the data in the larger size.

3   Set the title *Classes Form* in 14 point Verdana, Underlined.

4   Click on each control in turn and check its alignment. Left align controls for all fields except *Class No*, which should be right aligned.

Note: You can copy the formatting from one control to another using the **Format Painter** – select the control with the style you like, click the **Format Painter** button, and then click on another control to apply the same formatting to it.

Task 2: Borders, lines, alignment and fonts on reports

The last two tasks have involved forms. In this task you are required to apply borders, lines, alignment and fonts to a report.

Design a new report *Classes4* based on the *Classes* table. Format the report so that it looks like this.

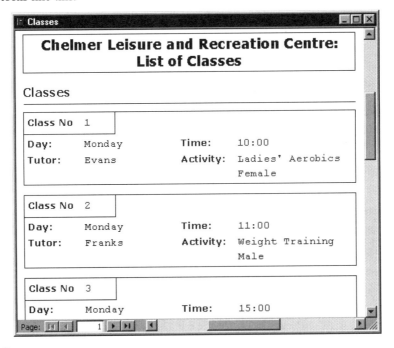

Figure 21.2

1   In the **Report Header** insert a label control and type in the title text shown above. Move the control to the centre, and centre align the text. Format the text to an appropriate font size and embolden it. Add a rectangle around the text.

2   In the **Page Header** section type in *Classes*. Format this text and place a line underneath it.

3   In the **Detail** section, add the controls and labels using the **Field List**. Click on the field list window title bar to select all fields, and then drag one of the fields to where you want the fields to start. Arrange the controls to roughly the layout shown above.

4   Edit the field names and format them as shown in the illustration.

5   Resize controls to fit the text in if necessary, and fine-tune their placement.

6   To align a group of controls select the group, right-click and choose **Align-Left/ Right/Top/Bottom**. Most of these controls are left and bottom aligned relative to each other.

7   Check the alignment of text within the controls. Ensure that all controls are left aligned.

8   Add a rectangle around the *Class No* controls. Add another rectangle to enclose all text in the Detail band.

9   At the top of the Page Footer band insert a line.

10   Preview the report, making sure that you have made your controls large enough to display their information (check the *Class Activity* in particular, because some of the entries, e.g. 'Body Conditioning', are quite long).

11   Make any necessary adjustments, preview again, and save the report as *Classes4*.

Special effects, colours and borders

What you will learn in this unit

You can make a control look three-dimensional, add colour or change border widths to make reports and forms look more interesting. Remember the design tips given in Unit 21 when adding colours and special effects to controls on printed reports – especially since most reports are likely to be printed in black and white.

By the end of this unit you will be able to:

❏ set colours

❏ set borders

❏ set 3-D effects.

Using the Formatting (Form/Report Design) toolbar

Special effects, colours and borders can be set using the Formatting (Form/Report Design) toolbar:

From left to right, these tools give you control over **Fill/Back**(ground) **Color**, **Font/Fore**(ground) **Color**, **Line/Border Color**, **Line/Border Width** and **Special Effects** (3D).

You can also set these properties through the Property Sheet. Double-click on the control or area to be changed and set the properties on the **Format** tab. Generally, it's easier to use the Formatting toolbar so we shall restrict ourselves to that here.

Back, fore and border colours

A control can have separate colours for background, foreground and border. To set a colour:

1   Select the control.

2   Click on the down arrow of the **Fill/Back Color** button to drop down the colour selection box, and choose a colour.

3   If the **Transparent** button in the colour selection box is clicked, the selected control is made transparent so that it shows whatever controls are behind it. This is usually what you want, and controls have a transparent background by default.

4   Repeat for **Font/Fore Color** and **Line/Border Color**.

5   Experiment with different colours until you have chosen a colour combination that is legible and draws attention to the right parts of the screen – test it on a black and white printer if necessary, as you may be surprised how little contrast there is between two apparently distinct colours when they're converted to greyscale!

Note: If you fill a rectangle with a back colour, it will obscure any controls underneath it, and you will need to use **Format-Send to Back** to make them visible again (see Unit 20).

Border widths

All controls have adjustable borders. Some, such as label controls have no border set as a default. Other controls, such as option groups, list boxes and combo boxes, have a thin black border as a default.

To select a border width, click on the drop-down arrow of the **Border Width** button on the toolbar. Choose a suitable border width from the options are shown (the numbers give the line thickness in points).

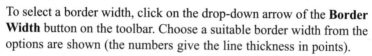

Special effects

There are six special effects to choose from: Flat, Raised, Sunken, Etched, Shadowed, and Chiselled. These options are displayed by clicking on the drop-down arrow of the **Special Effects** button on the toolbar. Rather than try to explain these in words, we recommend that you try each one in turn to see how it looks.

Using special effects with colours and borders

When you select any 3-D effect (i.e. not Flat), the 3-D effect is given the same colours as buttons on the toolbar and command buttons to achieve the effect. The 3-D effect colours are set by the Windows Control Panel, and you can only change the fore and back colours here. If you choose Shadowed, the back colour is the shadow colour.

If you change the border width on a 3-D control, it will revert to Flat; click the Special Effects to reapply the effect and remove the border.

Task 1: Setting dimensions and borders

Open the *Classes3* form and experiment with setting colours, borders and 3-D effects. For example, try:

1   Setting all the field labels as Raised.

2   Setting the Form Header as Sunken.

3   Increasing the width of the line in the Detail section.

4   Apply some colours to different parts of the screen to add interest.

Reviewing reports

What you will learn in this unit

This unit reviews and offers practice on the following topics:

❏ creating a single-column report using Report Wizards

❏ using and printing a single-column report

❏ creating a mailing label report.

Task 1: Creating a single-column report using Report Wizard

This task creates a single-column report for all of the properties in the *Properties* table, sorted in descending order according to selling price.

1 Using Report Wizards, create a report, resembling that shown in Figure 23.1, which shows the records for all of the properties in the database, including the following fields:

❏ Property No

❏ Address

❏ Town

❏ Selling Price

❏ Date of Entry.

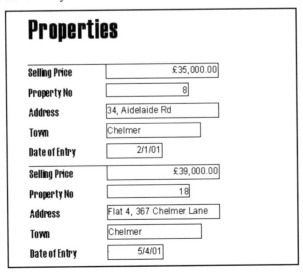

Figure 23.1 Single-column Properties report

2   Sort the records in descending order according to their selling price.

3   Choose a columnar layout for the report. Save the report as *Properties.*

Task 2: Using and printing a report

1   Select the report **Properties** and view it in preview.

2   Print from the preview screen or the design screen.

3   By choosing **File-Page Setup**, experiment with two or three columns (**Layout** tab) arranged across a landscape page (**Page** tab) as in Figure 23.2.

You may need to reduce the item size and column spacing as well as the margins of the page to fit in three columns.

Properties

Selling Price	£35,000.00		Selling Price	£39,000.00		Selling Price	£45,000.00
Property No	8		Property No	18		Property No	16
Address	34, Aidelaide Rd		Address	Flat 4, 367 Chelmer Lane		Address	Flat 1, Gracelands
Town	Chelmer		Town	Chelmer		Town	Woodford
Date of Entry	2/1/01		Date of Entry	5/4/01		Date of Entry	24/3/01
Selling Price	£45,000.00		Selling Price	£50,000.00		Selling Price	£55,000.00
Property No	5		Property No	2		Property No	4
Address	16, The Close		Address	56, Bodmin Drive		Address	2, Woodford Rd
Town	Branford		Town	Chelmer		Town	Meriton
Date of Entry	18/11/00		Date of Entry	20/9/00		Date of Entry	21/10/00
Selling Price	£60,000.00		Selling Price	£65,000.00		Selling Price	£67,000.00
Property No	14		Property No	15		Property No	19
Address	158, Moss Lane		Address	34, The Grove		Address	4, St Paul's Avenue
Town	Chelmer		Town	Chelmer		Town	Chelmer
Date of Entry	3/3/01		Date of Entry	15/3/01		Date of Entry	9/4/01

Figure 23.2

Task 3: Creating and using a mailing label report

This task asks you to create and use a mailing label report for a set of records selected from the database using a query. We wish to create a mailing label report that lists all detached properties.

1   Create a query that selects all records for detached houses. Include all fields. Save the query as *Detached*.

2   Create a mailing label report like the one in Figure 23.3 to include the records in the query dynaset and the following fields:

❑   Address

❑   Town

3   Include the text *The Occupier* at the top of each record.

4   Save the report as *Detached.*

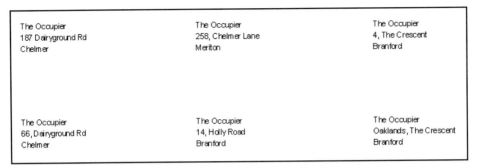

Figure 23.3 Mailing label report

Task 4: Customising a report

This task involves additional customisation of the *Properties* report created earlier in Task 1. The aim is to produce a report that looks similar to that in Figure 23.4.

1   Open the *Properties* report.

2   Move and size the controls on the *Properties* report so that they are positioned as in Figure 23.4.

3   Modify the size of the areas so that they just accommodate the appropriate text.

4   Modify the fonts, setting the type, size and style to match more closely the sample.

5   Add lines and rectangles to the report as shown.

6   Add borders to controls as indicated in Figure 23.4.

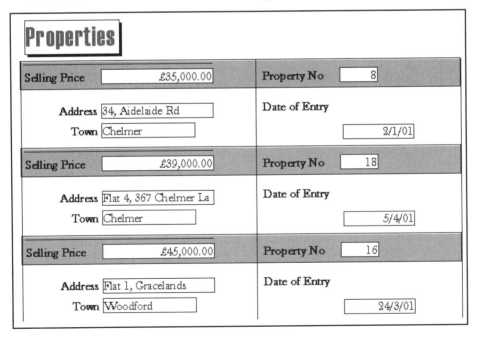

Figure 23.4 Customised Properties report

Relational databases

What you will learn in this unit

All the units so far have considered forms, queries and reports that are ultimately based on one table. A relational database management system, such as Access, allows more than one table to be created in a database and enables you to establish links between these tables, using common fields. This unit provides a brief introduction to the concept of a relational database and considers the advantages of storing data in separate files.

To explore how the Chelmer Leisure database can be developed into a relational database you should move on to *Access 2000 Further Skills*.

Understanding relationships between tables

We have created two databases, one concerning a leisure centre and the other an estate agency. Each database has one basic table, although a second table (Classes) has been included in the leisure centre database. However, if we were to consider all these businesses' functions then there may be much more data concerning different areas of the business that could be stored in the database. This is not an easy job in real life and is usually performed by systems analysts, who are trained in designing database systems to meet the needs of specific businesses.

Chelmer Leisure and Recreation Centre is one such business, although its operation and the information flows that these generate are much less complex than might be encountered in larger multinational business.

A leisure centre basically needs a building, staff and customers. Often it is cheaper to take out membership of a leisure centre than pay each time you go, and some centres require you to become a member before you can use their facilities. When someone joins the centre, details about that person, such as name and address, are obtained. Details about the staff who work at the centre will also be needed so that they can be paid correctly, e.g. name, salary and National Insurance number. Details about room, halls and courts bookings will be needed so that the building is used efficiently. Staff then know which facilities are being used and when, allowing for activity and room scheduling. In respect of the centre's bar or café inventory, details about stocks of food and drink would need to be kept as well as, for example, sales records.

Let's begin by reviewing membership data in more detail. What sort of information will the centre be asking for in the membership form? Apart from name and address, date of birth is useful for targeting advertising to specific groups, e.g. senior citizens, and knowing about members' sporting interests is also useful.

The information that Chelmer Leisure and Recreation Centre requires about each new member is shown in the following table:

Lastname	Occupation
Firstname	Date of Birth
Title	Date of joining
Street	Date of Last Renewal
Town	Sporting Interests
County	Smoker
Post Code	Sex
Telephone No	

The table contents are the names of each piece or field of information. Before issuing a membership card the centre will allocate a unique membership number, and will charge a membership fee. It offers different categories of membership for which different fees are charged.

The centre will need to hold data about the current fees charged for each category of membership. This would form another table in our system, the membership category table, which would have the following fields:

Category No
Category Type
Membership Fee

To discover the fee that a member has paid by matching his or her membership category with Category No in the membership category table (above), the information in the two tables can be linked. This is known as relating the tables, and by creating links between them, they appear to be one table.

One advantage of using more than one table is that less storage space is required. Consider the situation where there wasn't a membership category table and the information about category type and membership fee was stored in the table containing the member's information. If there are, say, 500 members, 500 membership category descriptions and 500 membership fee details must to be stored. However, with two tables there will be 500 category identification numbers in the main table, which need only be one digit, and if there are six categories, the second table will contain six category identification numbers, six descriptions and six fee details. Another advantage is that the fees can be amended and the new data is available throughout the database simultaneously, so that when a new member joins or membership is renewed the correct fee details are used. Since the membership and membership categories are related through the *Category No* field it is possible to create printed reports that include data from both tables.

We have already considered and created a table that can hold data concerning classes being held by the centre. Another table that could form part of the Chelmer Leisure and Recreation Centre system might refer to bookings of the rooms, halls and courts. The centre will need to keep track of room bookings to prevent double-booking and to schedule classes. Rooms can be booked either by members or by a class so there is one link between a member and a room booking, and another between a class and a room booking. The *Bookings* and *Classes* tables are shown below.

Bookings table	Classes table
Booking No	Class No
Room/Hall/Court	Class Day
Member/Class	Class Time
Member No	Class Tutor
Class No	Class Activity
Date	Male/Female/Mixed
Time	

Figure 24.1 shows the relational database that could be used by a system for Chelmer Leisure and Recreation Centre, and is in fact the one used in *Access 2000 Further Skills*. It shows how the four tables: *Membership*, *Membership Category*, *Classes* and *Bookings* are linked through common fields.

This is just one database structure that could be used for part of the system at Chelmer Leisure and Recreation Centre. The total system would be more complex and a number of alternative structures are possible. The best structure for a given application depends on the way in which the database is to be used or, more specifically, what information customers and managers need to be able to extract from it.

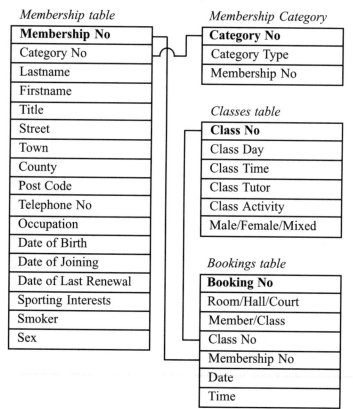

Figure 24.1 Chelmer Leisure and Recreation Centre Database

Task 1: Creating and linking tables

The Centre will need to have details of the class tutors that it employs. Design a *Tutors* table on paper by considering the fields that will comprise the records in this table. How could this table be linked in with the tables in Figure 24.1?

Queries and reports based on more than one table

If a relationship is defined between two or more tables, they can appear to act as one, and you can generate queries and reports from them. Creating a very simple relationship using the estate agency database will be considered in the next task.

Task 2: Creating a query and report based on linked tables

In this task you will create a table that lists the descriptions of house types and link it to the main table. You will then create query and report based on the two tables.

1   Open the *Chelmer Estates* database.

2   Create a table which lists the types of properties as illustrated below.

    1   Bungalow
    2   Detached
    3   Semi-detached
    4   Terraced
    5   Flat

3   Define the two fields, *House Type* (Number – Double) and *Description* (Text – 50). Save the table as *Property Type* without setting a primary key. Enter the data shown above and close the table.

4   Create a new query in Design view and add both tables. Click on the *House Type* field in the *Properties* table and drag it to the *House Type* field in the *Property Type* table. Access will draw a line between the two tables, indicating a link.

5   Add to the query the fields *Address*, *Town* and *Selling Price* from the *Properties* table, and *Description* from the *Property Type* table. Set a criterion to select properties below £75,000. View the query and save it as *Lower Priced Properties*. Create a report based on this query.

Summary

The aim of these units has been to introduce the basics of Access 2000, showing how to create a simple database, and to organise, select and print the data held within it. Using database management software may not be as easy to get to grips with as software such as word processors or spreadsheets, mainly because of the different components making up the database and the additional planning required to set it up. However, we hope you have enjoyed using Access. You will have noted from time to time references to the *Access 2000 Further Skills* text, which we strongly recommend you use to learn more about using Access.

Quick reference 1

Data for tables

Membership table data

Note that the Membership number is allocated automatically and cannot be edited. If you delete a record, you will lose that number, but this doesn't matter. If your numbers are different from those shown here, just make a note of the differences for reference with any tasks that use the numbers.

Membership no	Category	Lastname	Firstname	Title	Street
1	2	Walker	Andrew J	Mr	16 Dovecot Close
2	1	Simpson	Denise	Mrs	27 Bowling Green Rd
3	6	Perry	Jason R	Mr	59 Church Street
4	2	Forsythe	Ann M	Miss	2 Ferndale Close
5	1	Jameson	Donna	Mrs	25 Alder Drive
6	3	Robinson	Petra	Miss	16 Lowton Lane
7	5	Harris	David J	Mr	55 Coven Road
8	2	Shangali	Imran	Mr	47 High Street
9	1	Barrett	Martha A	Mrs	7 Oldcott Way
10	1	Weiner	George W F	Mr	6 Church Street
11	6	Ali	David	Mr	33 Meriton Road
12	2	Young	Aileen	Ms	78 Highgate Street
13	5	Gray	Ivor P	Mr	4 The Parade
14	5	Swift	Freda	Miss	23 Ferndale Close
15	1	Davies	Sandra M	Mrs	61 Hallfield Road
16	1	Robinson	Rebecca	Mrs	9 Moss Street
17	2	Everett	Alan	Mr	12 Stanley Street
18	4	Locker	Liam	Mr	2 Beech Close
19	4	Locker	Alison	Miss	2 Beech Close
20	1	Jones	Edward R	Mr	17 Mayfield Avenue

	Town	County	Post code	Telephone no	Occupation	Date of birth
1	Chelmer	Cheshire	CH2 6TR	01779 569234	Builder	12/3/52
2	Meriton	Cheshire	CH9 2EV	01779 552099	Housewife	29/11/60
3	Chelmer	Cheshire	CH1 8YU			3/6/82
4	Chelmer	Cheshire		01779 569945	Receptionist	5/8/73
5	Chelmer	Cheshire	CH2 7FN		Housewife	4/12/70

	Town	County	Post code	Telephone no	Occupation	Date of birth
6	Bradford	Staffs	ST10 2DZ	01778 890523		7/7/84
7	Chelmer	Cheshire	CH3 8PS	01779 569311	Retired	22/5/28
8	Chelmer	Cheshire	CH1 7JH	01779 561553	Accountant	15/3/55
9	Meriton	Cheshire	CH9 3DR	01779 557822	Teacher	25/11/60
10	Chelmer	Cheshire	CH1 8YV		Electrician	10/2/58
11	Chelmer	Cheshire	CH4 5KD	01779 569066		14/7/81
12	Branford	Staffs	ST10 4RT	01778 894471	Civil Servant	25/10/51
13	Chelmer	Cheshire	CH1 7ER	01779 565715	Unemployed	12/4/47
14	Chelmer	Cheshire	CH2 8PN	01779 567351	Retired	14/9/27
15	Meriton	Cheshire	CH9 1YJ	01778 891441	Clerk	1/2/65
16	Chelmer	Cheshire	CH2 8SE	01779 568812	Housewife	18/5/68
17	Chelmer	Cheshire	CH3 3CJ		Draughtsperson	30/7/57
18	Chelmer	Cheshire	CH3 8UH			30/12/83
19	Chelmer	Cheshire	CH3 8UH			30/12/83
20	Chelmer	Cheshire	CH2 90L	01779 567333	Bus Driver	22/12/58

	Date of joining	Date of last renewal	Sporting interests	Smoker	Sex
1	3/2/92	3/2/01	Tennis, squash	Yes	Yes
2	16/7/91	16/7/00	Aerobics, swimming, running, squash	No	No
3	12/12/96	12/12/00	Judo, karate	No	Yes
4	16/9/91	16/9/00		No	No
5	15/6/98	15/6/00	Aerobics, squash	Yes	No
6	3/5/94	3/1/01	Swimming, judo	No	No
7	1/2/99	1/2/01	Badminton, cricket	Yes	Yes
8	6/4/92	6/4/00	Weight training, squash	No	Yes
9	4/10/00	4/10/01	Keep fit, swimming	No	No
10	15/7/92	15/7/00	Weight training, squash	No	Yes
11	2/10/99	2/10/00	Judo, swimming, football	No	Yes
12	9/8/94	9/8/00	Keep fit, aerobics, squash	Yes	No
13	5/1/00	5/1/01		Yes	Yes
14	16/9/96	16/9/00		No	No
15	5/4/99	5/4/01	Aerobics, squash, swimming	Yes	No
16	6/12/98	6/12/00	Tennis, aerobics	No	No
17	5/11/94	5/11/00	Squash, fitness training, football	No	Yes
18	13/6/00	13/6/01		No	Yes
19	13/6/00	13/6/01		No	No
20	17/5/99	17/5/00	Weight training	Yes	Yes

Classes table data

Class no	Class day	Class time	Class tutor	Class activity	Male/female/mixed
1	Monday	10:00	Evans	Ladies' Aerobics	Female
2	Monday	11:00	Franks	Weight Training	Male
3	Monday	15:00	Latham	Body Conditioning	Mixed
4	Monday	19:00	Wheildon	Step Aerobics	Mixed
5	Tuesday	10:00	Jackson	Men's Multi-gym	Male
6	Tuesday	14:00	Adams	Ladies' Multi-gym	Female
7	Tuesday	19:00	Jackson	Family Multi-gym	Mixed
8	Wednesday	10:00	Evans	Ladies' Aerobics	Female
9	Wednesday	14:00	Latham	Body Conditioning	Mixed
10	Wednesday	15:00	Franks	Weight Training	Female
11	Wednesday	19:00	Franks	Weight Training	Mixed
12	Thursday	11:00	Latham	Weight Training	Male
13	Thursday	14:00	Wheildon	Step Aerobics	Mixed
14	Thursday	15:00	Adams	Multi-gym	Mixed
15	Thursday	19:00	Latham	Body Conditioning	Mixed
16	Friday	10:00	Latham	Body Conditioning	Female
17	Friday	11:00	Wheildon	Step Aerobics	Mixed
18	Friday	14:00	Jackson	Men's Multi-gym	Male

Estate Agency database – Properties table

Note that the Property Numbers are allocated by Access, so yours will differ from these if you delete records. You will notice that some numbers are different in the tasks as records are deleted while experimenting with this sample database.

Property No	Address	Town	House Type	No. of Bedrooms	Garage	Garden Length
1	3, Bude Close	Chelmer	3	4	1	40
2	56, Bodmin Drive	Chelmer	3	3	1	30
3	187, Dairyground Rd	Chelmer	2	4	2	80
4	2, Woodford Rd	Meriton	4	2	3	100
5	16, The Close	Branford	3	3	1	50
6	67, Steal Rd	Chelmer	3	5	1	75
7	258, Chelmer Lane	Meriton	2	3	1	120
8	34, Aidelaide Rd	Chelmer	5	1	1	0
9	345, Chelmer Lane	Chelmer	3	6	1	200
10	16, Park Road	Chelmer	1	4	2	250
11	4, The Crescent	Branford	2	6	2	300
12	66, Dairyground Rd	Chelmer	2	4	2	90
13	15, Pownall Lane	Chelmer	1	3	1	50
14	158, Moss Lane	Chelmer	1	2	1	60
15	34, The Grove	Chelmer	4	3	0	40
16	Flat 1, Gracelands	Woodford	5	2	0	0
17	14, Holly Road	Branford	2	7	2	500
18	Flat 4, 367 Chelmer Lane	Chelmer	5	1	1	0
19	4, St Paul's Avenue	Chelmer	3	3	1	70
20	Oaklands, The Crescent	Branford	2	5	2	150
21	18, Merrylands Lane	Branford	2	6	2	100

Property No	Leasehold/ Freehold	Selling price	Heating	Date of entry	Notes
1	Leasehold	£100,000	1	5/6/00	granny flat, listed, double glazing
2	Freehold	£50,000	2	20/9/00	triangular garden, integral garage, double glazing
3	Freehold	£111,000	2	1/10/00	cloakroom
4	Leasehold	£55,000	0	21/10/00	listed
5	Leasehold	£45,000	1	18/11/00	
6	Leasehold	£87,000	3	4/12/00	extended accommodation, in need of renovation

Property No	Leasehold/ Freehold	Selling price	Heating	Date of entry	Notes
7	Freehold	£89,000	1	15/12/00	listed thatched cottage, thoroughly renovated and modernised
8	Leasehold	£35,000	2	2/1/01	
9	Freehold	£150,000	4	5/1/01	
10	Freehold	£200,000	1	5/10/00	luxury home, cloakroom
11	Freehold	£300,000	1	12/12/00	luxury home, granny flat, cloakroom
12	Freehold	£115,000	2	2/1/01	granny flat
13	Freehold	£80,000	1	6/1/01	
14	Freehold	£60,000	2	3/3/01	
15	Leasehold	£65,000	0	15/3/01	in need of some additional renovation, listed
16	Freehold	£45,000	3	24/3/01	
17	Freehold	£400,000	4	26/3/01	rural property, with land and granny flat, cloakroom
18	Leasehold	£39,000	2	5/4/01	
19	Freehold	£67,000	1	9/4/01	
20	Freehold	£250,000	1	26/4/01	
21	Freehold	£120,000	1	15/5/01	

Data definitions

Classes table

Name		Type	Size
Class No	*Index*: Primary key	AutoNumber	4
Class Day	*Required*: True	Text	10
Class Time	*Required*: True	Date/Time	8
	Format: hh:mm	Short time	
Class Tutor	*Index*: Ascending	Text	30
Class Activity	*Required*: True	Text	20
	Index: Ascending		
Male/Female/Mixed	*Validation Rule*: "Male" or "Female" or "Mixed"	Text	
	Validation Text: Please enter Male, Female or Mixed		

Membership table

Name		Type	Size
Membership No	*Description*: Automatic membership numbering *Index*: Primary key	AutoNumber	4
Category No	*Description*: Categories are 1-Senior, 2-Senior Club, 3-Junior, 4-Junior Club, 5-Concessionary, 6-Youth Club *Validation Rule*: <=6 *Validation Text*: Please enter a category between 1 and 6 *Required*: True	Number (Byte)	1
Lastname	*Required*: True *Index*: Lastname+Firstname	Text	25
Firstname	*Index*: Lastname+Firstname	Text	30
Title		Text	10
Street	*Required*: True	Text	30
Town	*Default value*: Chelmer *Required*: True	Text	25
County	*Default value*: Cheshire *Required*: True	Text	20
Post Code	*Format:*>	Text	20
Telephone No		Text	12
Occupation		Text	50

Name		Type	Size
Date of Birth	*Format*: Short Date	Date/Time	8
Date of Joining	*Format*: Short Date	Date/Time	8
Date of Last Renewal	*Format*: Short Date	Date/Time	8
Sporting Interests		Memo	0
Smoker	*Format*: ;"Smoker";"Non-Smoker"	Yes/No	1
Sex	*Format*: ;"Male";"Female"	Yes/No	1

Quick reference 2

Basic Windows operations

If you have not previously used Windows, you are strongly recommended to run through the tutorial that is supplied as part of the Windows package to introduce new users to Windows. Though Windows comes in many varieties, the key operations are the same in the 97, 2000, Me and NT editions.

This appendix briefly summarises some of the key operations and should act as a ready reference to some of the terminology that is used elsewhere in the book.

Mouse pointer shapes

When the mouse is pointed at different parts of the screen, the pointer shape changes to show it is ready to perform different tasks. Some commands also change the pointer shape.

This table lists some common pointer shapes as encountered in Access.

Pointer	Meaning
I	The pointer is over a text area. Click to position an insertion point where text may be typed.
⌂	The pointer appears over menus, non-text areas of windows, inactive windows, scroll bars or toolbars. You can choose from a menu or click a button. You can use the pointer to drag (hold down the left mouse button while you draw an area on-screen, then release the button) to make a selection.
⇧	The pointer is over the edge of a cell. You can select the cell now.
⧖	Access is performing a task that will take a few seconds.
⊹	Appears along the borders between window sections or columns
‡	Drag to resize the section or row.
⌂?	The Help pointer appears after you press _Shift+F1_. You can now point to any item on the screen and click to view specific Help.
⬌	This pointer appears when you have selected **Move** or **Size** from the **Control** menu. You can move the window to a new position or drag the window border.
↓	This pointer appears over the grey bar at the top of a column in a table, query or filter. Click to select the column.

➡️ This pointer appears in the record selection bar. Click to select the record.

🔖 This is the drag and drop pointer, which appears when you make a selection, drag the selection to its new location and release the mouse button to drop or insert the selection.

🔍 This is the zoom pointer which appears in print preview, allowing you to magnify and reduce the size of the on-screen preview.

↔↕↖↗ The pointer is on the sizing handle of a window or a control. The shape varies according to the handle. Drag to resize the object.

✋ ✏️ In form or report design this pointer is used to move an individual label or control.

✋ In form or report design this pointer is used to move a label and control pair, or a selected group of controls.

+ This pointer appears next to a Toolbox icon and indicates the position of the control on the form or report design. Click to position the control.

Basics of Windows: a Quick Review

The Windows screen has the following features.

Menu bar

The menu bar shows the titles of the various pull-down menus that are available with a given application. To select a menu option, first select the menu by placing the mouse pointer over the name of the menu on the menu bar and click the left mouse button. The menu will appear. Move the mouse pointer to the menu option you require and click the left mouse button again. Note that any menu options displayed in light grey are not currently available. Menus can also be accessed via the keyboard: press the *Alt* key together with the underlined letter of the menu option, e.g. to select the **File** menu press *Alt+F*.

Control menu

The Control menu is found on all application and document windows. To access it, click on the Control Menu icon in the far left of the title bar, or press *Alt+Spacebar*. The exact contents are different for different windows, but typically include such basic window operations as Restore, Move, Size, Minimize, Maximize and Close.

Maximize, minimize and restore buttons

Clicking on the Maximize button ▣ enlarges a window to its maximum size, so that it fills the whole desktop.

Clicking on the Minimize button ▣ reduces the window to an icon on the Taskbar. When you shrink an application window to an icon, the application is still running in memory, but its window is not taking up space on your desktop.

Clicking on the **Restore** button ⊟ will restore a minimized or maximized window to its previous size.

Clicking on the **Close** button ⊠ closes the window.

Title bar

The title bar tells you which window is displayed. You can move a window by dragging on its title bar (as long as the window is not maximized, i.e. not taking up the whole screen).

Taskbar

At the bottom of your screen is the Taskbar. It contains the **Start** button, which you use to quickly start a program, find a file, or get Help. Beside the Start button you will probably see some small icons which are used to get to common applications quickly.

When you start an application, a button appears on the task bar with the name of the application and current document name (if a document is open). You can use this button to switch between the application windows you have open.

Dialog boxes

Windows uses dialog boxes to request information from you, and to provide information to you. Most dialog boxes include options, with each option asking for a different kind of information.

After all the requested information has been supplied, you choose a command button to carry out the command. Two that feature on every dialog box are **OK** and **Cancel**. **OK** causes the command to be executed, **Cancel** cancels the operation and removes the dialog box from the screen. These buttons represent the two means of quitting from a dialog box. To choose a command button, click on it, or if the button is currently active (highlighted by a thickened border), press the _Enter_ key.

There are a number of different kinds of controls found in dialog boxes.

❑   Text boxes are where you can type in text, such as a filename. The presence of a flashing vertical bar, or the insertion point, indicates that the text box is active and that you may enter text. If the text box is not active, place the mouse pointer on the box and click. The insertion point will then appear in the box.

❑   List boxes show a column of available choices. Items can usually be selected from a list box by clicking on the item; in some situations you may need to double-click.

❑   Check boxes are used to control options that you can switch on and off. You can select as many or as few check box options as are applicable. When an option in a check box is selected it contains a ✓ ; otherwise the box is empty. To select a check box, click on the empty box.

❑   Radio buttons appear as a set of mutually exclusive options – you can select only one at a time, though this can be changed by selecting a different button. The selected button contains a black dot. To select a radio button, click on it.

❑ Scroll bars appear at the side of windows and list boxes. They appear when the information contained in a window cannot be displayed wholly within that window. Both vertical and horizontal scroll bars may be present, depending on whether the contents of the window are too long or too wide to fit inside it.

The small block in the middle of the bar represents the position of the currently displayed portion of the whole object. You can move to a different position in the object by moving this block. You can move it either by clicking on the scroll bar arrow boxes, clicking on the scroll bar itself, or by dragging the block.

Quick reference 3

Access Toolbars

Access window

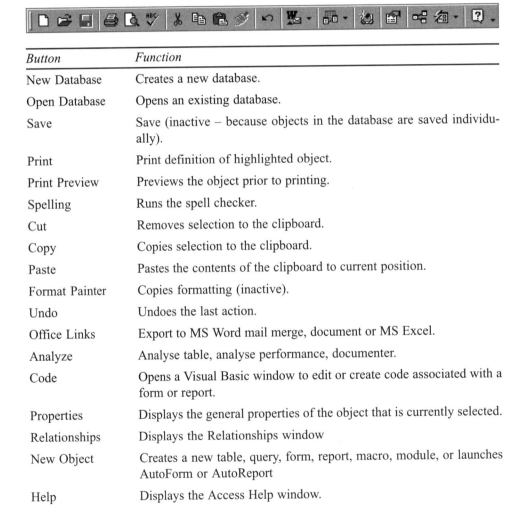

Button	Function
New Database	Creates a new database.
Open Database	Opens an existing database.
Save	Save (inactive – because objects in the database are saved individually).
Print	Print definition of highlighted object.
Print Preview	Previews the object prior to printing.
Spelling	Runs the spell checker.
Cut	Removes selection to the clipboard.
Copy	Copies selection to the clipboard.
Paste	Pastes the contents of the clipboard to current position.
Format Painter	Copies formatting (inactive).
Undo	Undoes the last action.
Office Links	Export to MS Word mail merge, document or MS Excel.
Analyze	Analyse table, analyse performance, documenter.
Code	Opens a Visual Basic window to edit or create code associated with a form or report.
Properties	Displays the general properties of the object that is currently selected.
Relationships	Displays the Relationships window
New Object	Creates a new table, query, form, report, macro, module, or launches AutoForm or AutoReport
Help	Displays the Access Help window.

Database window

Button	Function
Open	Opens or runs the selected database object.
Design	Opens the selected object in Design view.
New	New form, report, table, etc.
Delete	Delete selected database object.
Large icons	Displays database objects in large icons. Icons can be dragged anywhere in the window, like icons on a desktop.
Small icons	Displays database objects in small icons.
List	Displays database objects with small icons in columns (layout cannot be changed).
Details	Lists database objects with details such as file size and creation date.

Table design view

Button	Function
View	Displays the data in the table in the form of a datasheet.
Save	Saves the table.
Print	Print (inactive).
Print Preview	Print preview (inactive).
Spelling	Spell check (inactive).
Cut	Removes selection to the clipboard.
Copy	Copies selection to the clipboard.
Paste	Pastes the contents of the clipboard to current position.
Format Painter	Copies formatting (inactive).
Undo	Undoes the last action.
Primary Key	Sets primary key for selected field(s).
Indexes	Displays the Indexes dialog box.
Insert Rows	Inserts a row above the current row.
Delete Rows	Deletes the current row(s).
Properties	Displays properties of table.
Build	Displays a tool for defining the selected item or property, often as an expression (only enabled if builder available).
Database window	Displays the Database window.
New Object	Creates a new table, query, form, report, macro, module, or launches AutoForm or AutoReport.
Help	Displays the Access Help window.

Query design view

Button	Function
View mode	Displays the data in the query in the form of a datasheet.
Save	Saves the query.
Print	Print (inactive).
Print Preview	Print preview (inactive).
Spelling	Spell check (inactive).
Cut	Removes selection to the clipboard.
Copy	Copies selection to the clipboard.
Paste	Pastes the contents of the clipboard to current position.
Format Painter	Copies formatting (inactive).
Undo	Undoes the last action.
Query Type	Drop-down list for the type of query: Select Query (default type), Crosstab query for summarising data, Make Table query, Update query, Append query or Delete query.
Run	Runs the query.
Show Table	Displays the Show Table dialog box for adding tables to a query.
Totals	Displays total row in QBE grid for statistical summary.
Top Values	Finds the top values in the active query based on a percentage or number of rows.
Properties	Displays the properties of the query.
Build	Displays the Expression builder.
Database window	Displays the Database window.
New Object	Creates a new table, query, form, report, macro, module, or launches AutoForm or AutoReport.
Help	Displays the Access Help window.

Datasheet and form view

Button	Function
Design view	Displays table in Design view for modification.
Save	Saves the table layout.
Print	Prints the datasheet.
Print Preview	Displays a print preview.
Spelling	Spell check.
Cut	Removes selection to the clipboard.

Copy	Copies selection to the clipboard.
Paste	Pastes from the clipboard to current position.
Format Painter	Copies formatting (inactive).
Undo	Undoes the last action.
Insert Hyperlink	Inserts or modifies a hyperlink address.
Sort Ascending	Displays records in ascending order of current field.
Sort Descending	Displays records in descending order of current field.
Filter by Selection	Filters records based on selected data.
Filter by Form	Displays a form for the entry of filter criteria.
Apply Filter	Displays filtered records.
Find	Search for selected data.
New Record	Go to new record.
Delete Record	Removes record.
Database window	Displays the Database window.
New Object	Creates a new table, query, form, report, macro, module, or launches AutoForm or AutoReport.
Help	Displays the Access Help window.

Form design view

Top row

Button	Function
View	Runs the form.
Save	Saves the form.
Print	Prints the form.
Print Preview	Displays the print preview.
Spelling	Spell check (inactive).
Cut	Removes selection to the clipboard.
Copy	Copies selection to the clipboard.
Paste	Pastes from the clipboard to current position.
Format Painter	Copies formatting from one control to another; double-click to copy to several controls, *Esc* to finish.
Undo	Undoes the last action.
Insert Hyperlink	Inserts or modifies a hyperlink address.
Field List	Displays the field list window.
Toolbox	Displays the Toolbox as a window or toolbar.

AutoFormat	Applies your choice of predefined formats to the form.
Code	Displays an Access Basic form module in the Module window.
Properties	Displays the properties sheet.
Build	Displays a builder for the selected item or property (only enabled if builder available).
Database window	Displays Database window.
New Object	Creates a new table, query, form, report, macro, module, or launches AutoForm or AutoReport.
Help	Displays the Access Help window.

Bottom row

Button	Function
Object	Select a section of a form, a control, or the entire form.
Font	Drop-down list of fonts.
Font Size	Drop-down list of font sizes.
Bold	Applies bold typeface.
Italic	Applies italic typeface.
Underline	Applies underlining.
Align Left	Aligns contents of label or control to the left.
Center	Centres contents of label or control.
Align Right	Aligns contents of label or control to the right.
Fill/Back Color	Drop-down background colour selection.
Font/Fore Color	Drop-down foreground colour selection.
Line/Border Color	Drop-down border colour selection.
Line/Border Width	Drop-down border width selection.
Special Effect	Drop-down special effect (raised, sunken, etc.) selection.

Report design view

Top row

Button	Function
View	Previews report.
Save	Saves the report.
Print	Prints report.
Print Preview	Displays a print preview.
Spelling	Spell check (inactive).

Cut	Removes selection to the clipboard.
Copy	Copies selection to the clipboard.
Paste	Pastes from the clipboard to current position.
Format Painter	Copies formatting from one control to another; double-click to copy to several controls, _Esc_ to finish.
Undo	Undoes the last action.
Insert Hyperlink	Inserts or modifies a hyperlink address.
Field List	Displays the Field list window.
Toolbox	Displays the Toolbox window.
Sorting and grouping	Displays the Sorting and Grouping dialog box.
AutoFormat	Applies your choice of predefined formats to the report.
Code	Displays an Access Basic report module in the Module window.
Properties	Displays the properties sheet.
Build	Displays a builder for the selected item or property (only enabled if builder available).
Database window	Displays Database window.
New Object	Creates a new table, query, form, report, macro, module, or launches AutoForm or AutoReport.
Help	Displays the Access Help window.

Bottom row

Button	Function
Object	Select a section of a report, a control, or the entire report.
Font Name	Drop-down list of fonts.
Font Size	Drop-down list of font sizes.
Bold	Applies bold typeface.
Italic	Applies italic typeface.
Underline	Applies underlining.
Align Left	Aligns contents of label or control to the left.
Center	Centres contents of label or control.
Align Right	Aligns contents of label or control to the right.
Fill/Back Color	Drop-down background colour selection.
Font/Fore Color	Drop-down foreground colour selection.
Line/Border Color	Drop-down border colour selection.
Line/Border Width	Drop-down border width selection.
Special Effect	Drop-down special effect (raised, sunken, etc.) selection.

Report and form print preview

Button	Function
View	Displays report or form in Design view for modification.
Print	Print.
Zoom	Zoom in or out.
One Page	Displays print preview one-page format.
Two Pages	Displays print preview two-page format.
Multiple pages	Displays print preview multiple-page format.
Zoom	Controls the amount of magnification.
Close	Closes preview and returns to design.
OfficeLinks	**Merge It with MS Word**: Merges the output of a table, query, form, report or module with a Word document – to insert names and addresses into a form letter, for instance.
	Publish It with MS Word: Displays the output of a table, query, form, report or module as a Word document.
	Analyze It with MS Excel: Displays the output of a table, query, form, report or module as a n Excel spreadsheet.
Database window	Displays the Database window.
New Object	Creates a new table, query, form, report, macro, module, or launches AutoForm or AutoReport.
Help	Displays the Access Help window.

Glossary

Access	A relational database product.
Alignment	When applied to a group of controls, this refers to their position relative to each other. When applied to a single control, it refers to the position of text within the control frame.
Case sensitive	Distinguishing between upper and lower case text.
Check boxes	Boxes offering a list of options which you can switch on or off.
Control	An individual design element of a report or form.
Control menu	The menu found on all windows accessed by clicking on the Control Menu icon in the far left of the title bar.
Data type	The type of data allowed in a particular field.
Database	A collection of related data.
DataBase Management System (DBMS)	Software used to manipulate and present data stored in a computer.
Database window	The principal window of a database, giving you access to all the tables, queries and other database objects within it.
Datasheet view	The view in which you can view and enter data in tables.
Default value	A value entered automatically by Access in a field in a new record.
Design view	The view in which you can create and modify tables, forms, reports and queries.
Detail	The detail section of a form or report, i.e. the actual data from records in a database.
Dialog box	A box used to request or provide information.
Dynaset	A temporary table produced as the result of a query.
Field	A piece of data within a record.
Field description	The description of a field. It may be up to 255 characters long.
Field list	A list of fields that a form was based upon.
Field name	The name of a field. Field names can be up to 64 characters including spaces. Full stops (.), exclamation marks (!) and square brackets ([ ]) are not allowed.
Field properties	Detailed definitions of a data type.

Filter	A means of displaying selected records.
Font	The style of text, like a typeface in printing.
Form	An on-screen method of collecting information for a database.
Group footer	A section marking the end of a group in a report.
Group header	A section marking the beginning of a group in a report.
Grouped report	A report with selected fields placed in a row. Records are grouped according to the value of a field in the table or query.
List boxes	Boxes showing a column of available choices.
Mailing label reports	Reports for creating mailing labels.
Make table query	A kind of query which selects data from a table (or more than one) and creates a new table from that data.
Maximize button	The button that enlarges a window to its maximum size.
Menu bar	The bar showing titles of various pull-down menus that are available in an application.
Minimize button	The button that reduces a window to a small icon at the bottom of the screen.
Module	Programs or sets of instructions designed to perform a specific task or series of tasks.
Null value	An empty field.
Option buttons	A list of mutually exclusive items on a form, only one of which can be selected by a user.
Page footer	A section that appears at the bottom of every page of a report.
Page header	A section that appears at the top of each page of a report such as a running title and page number.
Preview	An on-screen preview of how a page will look when printed.
Primary key	A field or combination of fields that uniquely identifies a record.
Properties sheet	A list of properties of a component of a form or report, which determine its appearance, behaviour and the data it holds.
Queries	A method of asking questions of a database.
Query criteria	The method of framing questions to allow specific records to be retrieved from the database.
Query Design window	The window from which you design a query.
Record	A set of details about an individual item. Each item has a separate record in the table.
Report footer	A section that appears at the very end of a report.
Report header	A section that appears at the very beginning of a report.

Report	Collection of data, usually the result of a query, designed and formatted for printing.
Restore button	The button that restores a minimized or maximized window to its previous size.
Row selector symbols	Symbols at the edge of a table row, which you click on to select a row of information.
Screen form	Interfaces which give access to the tables and queries in a database in a user-friendly way, instead of directly in Datasheet view.
Scroll bars	Bars which appear at the side of windows and list boxes when all the information cannot be displayed within the window. They allow you to scroll through the information.
Single-column form	A form which allows the user to input one record at a time.
Single-column report	A report with all selected fields in a single column.
String	A collection of characters (letters, numbers, and punctuation marks) that make up the data in a field.
Table Design window	The interface that allows you to define the structure of your table.
Tables	The primary building block of a database – a table holds data in a grid, where each column holds a particular kind of information about an item, and each row holds a different item.
Tabular form	A form which displays more than one record on the screen.
Task bar	The bar at the bottom of the screen containing the Windows Start button and buttons for active windows.
Text boxes	Boxes which allow you to type in text.
Title bar	Top section of a window containing the name of the window. Changes colour to indicate whether the window is active or inactive.
Toolbox	A selection of tools with which controls and text are added to a form or report.
Validation rules	Tests used to detect mistakes in data entry.
Wizards	Series of dialog boxes which help you create forms, reports, etc. using preset values.
Zero length string	"" empty quotes, used to indicate that there is no data for the field in that record.

Index